No Easy Road

No Easy Road

Patsy Whyte

Kailyard Publishing

First published in the United Kingdom in 2009
by Kailyard Publishing

ISBN 978-0-9563566-0-4
Produced by
The Choir Press
www.thechoirpress.co.uk

Dedication

For Mum and Dad, James, Georgina, Mary Anne, Lottie, John, Billy, Michael, Andy and Alec. Their road was as difficult as my own.

This book is also dedicated to my partner John, and to Jacqueline, Ian, Kimberley, Samantha and Lucinda, my lovely children.

Acknowledgements

I would like to thank everyone at The Choir Press for their kindness and true professionalism shown at all times. In particular, I'd like to mention Miles Bailey, Rachel Woodman and Irene Wood. Nothing was ever too much trouble for them. What wonderful people you are. Thank you!

Chapter One

I WAS ONLY FOUR when I had my first vision. It wasn't a dream. I was wide awake at the time. It happened in the small dingy cloakroom of a children's home in Aberdeen. A short while before, the cloak-room had been crammed full of noisy kids putting on coats and jackets prior to leaving for school. Now it was quiet. The long line of hooks to hang up the coats and jackets was empty. There was only one little red coat, my coat, left hanging on its own.

It was still early morning. I listened to the sharp clatter of break-fast plates being gathered up in the dining room ready for washing in the old stone sink in the kitchen next door. Outside, the rain poured down. It was a miserable day but I longed to go out and play in the large playground where the hamster lived. The hamster lived down a drain but so far I'd never seen him. The big boys told me he was there and I believed them. Every day, I poked a stick down the drain and scraped the muck at the bottom looking for him. But he never appeared and my brown woollen jumper and tartan trousers were caked in mud and dirt. I must have looked a sight, judging by the expression of horror on Edith's face. She worked at the home and always called me in when it was time for lunch. First, she had to clean me up, which she hated doing.

The morning dragged on and I became more and more restless sitting on the only chair in the cloakroom, swinging my legs backwards and forwards. I jumped off to look out through the long narrow cloakroom windows. Nothing had changed except the raindrops, which were bigger, hitting off the panes of glass even harder than before.

I peered through the sheets of rain and out across the playground to the high red brick wall at the back of the home. Suddenly, the wall crumbled away before my eyes. I was no longer in the gloomy cloakroom with its cracked and flaking paint but on an empty beach, running barefoot on wet sand at the water's edge. A cooling, gentle breeze played across my face and a feeling of pure joy rose within me. I heard the soothing sound of waves lapping at my side and the cry of gulls as they soared high into the clear blue sky above me. Nothing can touch me, I thought, as I ran and ran and ran.

Then my eyes focused for a moment on a small white cottage barely a speck in the distance. In the next instant, it was there, right in front of me, homely and inviting. The front door was open slightly, leading into a warm and cheerful hallway with white wallpaper covered in small red roses. I knew there was someone waiting inside for me but as I stepped through the doorway everything changed. The red brick wall formed again and I was back in the cloakroom looking out the window at the pouring rain.

The vision, which I still remember clearly to this day, left a profound impression on me. The beach was everything I longed for, the space and freedom I didn't have living with 18 other children at the home. What was it about the wallpaper which so caught my attention? It might have been the sheer living beauty of the roses. And who was waiting for me? I still don't know, but I am certain there really was somebody in the cottage.

I never told anyone about my vision. It was a magical moment meant just for me and it didn't matter whether I understood it or not. I just accepted it, the way a young child does.

⚬⚬

It took me over 40 years to reach this moment in time. Shortly, I would learn a little about the earliest years of my life and perhaps even discover the reason why I was taken into care. I felt nervous, even a little scared. The two men sitting down with me were social workers, strangers, whom I'd only talked to briefly on the telephone. A new law was in force and now I could look at the file which the authorities kept on me while I was in care. That was why I was here, in a modern and spacious council office five floors up in the middle of Glenrothes. The office had large gleaming windows looking out towards Falkland Hill in the distance and the enormous swathe of Fife lying in between. The sun shone brightly through the glass panes, making the office feel slightly too warm for comfort.

One of the social workers left the room and returned a few seconds later carrying an old folder. He placed it gently on the large polished table in front of me. The folder had a strong musty smell and was yellowing with age, and looked like it had been buried in some dusty filing cabinet for years until this moment. It was never meant to see the light of day.

I opened the folder with trembling hands and touched the untidy collection of papers inside. None of them were in any kind of order. They looked old and forgotten, destined never to belong to me. Yet they were all about me, the key which might unlock my early life and roots and answer the questions still haunting me even after so many years. Picking up a page and reading it felt like biting on forbidden fruit. The two social workers sat quietly watching me and I sensed their discomfort. This was a new experience for us all. My mouth was dry and the only sound I heard was my heart pounding in my ears. Everything else in the room disappeared into the background.

Words like pneumonia, gastroenteritis, verminous, puny, jumped out from the page, describing a child of 19 months I now felt no connection with. She was a stranger. The more senior of the two social workers broke the silence after spreading some of the papers on the table.

"Would you mind if I looked at this, Patricia?" he asked, holding up a crumpled piece of paper. "It's just that I've never seen something as old as this before."

I couldn't take in what I was reading. My eyes flitted from word to word, from top to middle to bottom of the page and then up again, in no logical order. I was trying to keep my emotions in check but the tears welling up inside made it hard to concentrate. No, I'm not going to cry in front of them, I said over and over to myself. Taking slow, deep breaths, I composed myself and lifted up my head slightly and looked at the social worker.

"No, go ahead, I don't mind," I said quietly.

I picked up an old school report filled with unflattering comments. *Patricia is a dreamer ... doesn't try hard enough ... head in the clouds ... Patricia's not very bright ...* The senior social worker asked if he could read it.

Then he looked at me sympathetically and said, "You know Patricia, most kids brought up in care never did very well."

"I suppose it's true. I certainly wasn't too bright." Old memories flooded back. The never-ending taunts of a "homey kid" made me stand out from the other kids. I felt ashamed of who I was and where I lived. I didn't want to know much about school after that.

The file contained small memos, records of telephone conversations and messages passed between social workers. The words "wanted by the police" carelessly scribbled in pencil on one of them stood out. But I was no criminal. I was 15 at the time and deeply unhappy after years trapped in the care system. I wanted out. When the police caught me after four days on the run, I was returned to Aberdeen in handcuffs.

The senior social worker asked me if there was anything I wanted to talk about. He was being kind, doing his best to help me through a difficult afternoon. I told him no, there wasn't. How could I explain in a mere handful of words how I felt when I didn't really know myself? I wasn't ready to confront the pain and injustice of my long years of loneliness in the children's home. I didn't want to remember the teenage years which followed. They were hard miserable years and I paid dearly for all the mistakes I made. But I was lucky, even as I struggled to make sense of a world without family or friends around me for support. I survived, somehow.

The afternoon was all but gone and many questions had been answered. Not all of them, but I knew now I was ill in hospital with pneumonia and gastroenteritis and then taken into care as soon as I recovered. The Aberdeen authorities thought they were saving me from a life of poverty and squalor.

The papers were gathered up from the table and placed carefully back in the file. Soon, it would be returned once more to the dusty filing cabinet from where it came and forgotten about. It was time to leave.

"You proved them all wrong, no matter what they wrote about you," said the senior social worker, shaking my hand. "It would have been nice if the file had told you something about your roots."

He was right. His words kept spinning around in my mind as the lift descended to the ground floor. The doors opened and I stepped into a busy foyer bustling with activity. It was a relief to be back in the present. I left the building and stood in front of it for a few minutes, pondering on the events of the afternoon. I was lost in thought. People passed me by wondering what I was doing. The rush hour started but I hardly noticed. The file told part of the story of my earliest years but so many pieces of the jigsaw were still missing. I had to find out more.

By coincidence, I was just begining to build up a long-distance telephone relationship with my sister Mary Anne, who lived in a remote cottage in the Scottish Highlands with her husband. I remembered meeting her for the first time when I was four. No one told me who she was or that she was my sister. It wasn't considered important enough. When we met again in 1996, at my dad's funeral, more than thirty years had passed. We crossed paths for only the third time in our lives at my mum's funeral, a short while after. So we talked a lot on the telephone. We had so much to catch up on.

๑๖๖

I was born in a former army barracks in 1955. That much I already knew from my birth certificate. Castlehill Barracks was the home of the Gordon Highlanders until they left in 1935. The barracks was taken over by Aberdeen Corporation and later used to house traveller families. I lived there for the first nineteen months of my life and Mary Anne for eleven years.

Home for most of the year was two small adjoining damp rooms with bare walls and floorboards and a single gas lamp for lighting. Nine of us lived in the rooms including my mum and dad. There was no electricity or hot water to wash with or to keep clothes clean and only one double bed, which we children all slept in.

Jobs were scarce and my dad turned his hand to just about anything to earn a shilling or two. Sometimes he found work at sea on the trawlers or he and mum would go hawking around the doors, selling old clothes and anything else they picked up in the market in the Castlegate. When spring arrived, we all piled on the back of a horse and cart and travelled the countryside for weeks on end. Sometimes we met up with other travellers, either on the road or at the traditional camping grounds, where we exchanged news and told stories and sang songs around the camp fire.

For many years, I was puzzled by a recurring vision which I could never explain. In the vision, I saw a young woman, standing tall and straight, her long black hair blowing in the wind. She stood silhouetted against the sky and the rolling hills in the distance. There was always a sense of happiness with her. I knew she loved the freedom and the emptiness all around her.

Then, quite by chance, a book I was reading had a photograph in it showing the traditional traveller camping ground at the Bay of Nigg, just outside Aberdeen. There was something familiar about the photograph which I couldn't put my finger on. I was certain I'd never been there before. As I casually traced the outline of the distant hills with my fingertips, I suddenly realised they were the same as the hills in my vision.

Now I understood what I was seeing all those years. The vision was actually my earliest memory, a fragment of that summer in 1956 when it was still possible to experience the traveller way of life. The woman in the vision was my mum.

When the summer was over, we returned home because the law demanded all traveller children should attend school for 200 days out of every year. The miserable conditions at the barracks gradually grew worse over the winter months until they finally took their toll. The day I was taken into hospital was the last day we would ever spend together as a family. "The Cruelty" called shortly afterwards and took all my brothers and sisters into care.

❧

Seven years later, as I walked through the Castlegate on the way to the Salvation Army's Citadel mission hall with my cousin Anne, I knew little about my family, or Castlehill Barracks, even although it lay only a short distance away. We were happy to escape the children's home for a couple of hours and sing for the down-and-outs who gathered at the Citadel every evening. The air was filled with a strange odour, a mixture of decay, poverty and cheap wine, which I didn't recognise at the time. The down-and-outs were hungry and desperate and had no option but to endure endless prayers and our hymn singing if they wanted a hot bowl of soup and a bed for the night. In the morning, they'd be thrown out into the street again to face another hopeless day.

I didn't understand any of that at the time. All I saw was the old man with the matted yellow hair and weather-beaten red cheeks sitting in the front row of the hall. Now and again, he looked up from the precious bowl of soup cradled in his dirty hands to the small stage where we stood, neatly dressed for the occasion. Each time our eyes met and locked for a brief second, a fleeting, nervous smile crossed his face. As the smile turned to a wide grin, a gaping chasm opened up revealing a mouth with not a single tooth in it. A second later, his head dropped down to the bowl and the loud slurping sound everyone was trying hard to ignore rose once more above the sound of singing. It was all but impossible to praise the Lord in between the slurping noises and Anne warbling out of tune next to me. My feeble attempts at singing finally turned into fits of laughter. I couldn't take my eyes off the old man's face. It was now contorted and misshapen as he struggled to chew on a slice of hard crusty bread. I found it all so funny.

I couldn't help thinking about the old man on the way back to the children's home. There was something about his eyes which made me feel very sad. I didn't mean to laugh. It was just the reaction of innocence. Little did I know one day, in the not too distant future, I would be where he was now, walking the same path and feeling rejected and alone and struggling to survive in a heartless world.

Chapter Two

I FEARLESSLY LAUNCHED the little three-wheeler bike down the small grassy mound, tightly gripping the handlebars. My long wavy hair lifted and billowed out in the air behind me. Ahead was a grand old white painted house. The scent of heavily ripe apples hung in the air. All around me was the sound of children laughing. But I barely registered them. I was happy to be in the warm sunshine in my own little world.

The bike came to a halt and I felt a sharp tug on my hair. I turned around to see a cheeky little black-haired boy looking back at me. It was Alan.

"Go away!" I shouted out.

He didn't stop. Instead, he teased me all the more, pulling harder at my hair. It felt painful. I lost my temper and started to cry. Alan ran away.

It was now the middle of the afternoon. A lady was gently leading me by the hand down a winding path where rays of sunshine sparkled through tall bushy trees. As we walked, she sang "Teddy Bear's Picnic" over and over and over. I wouldn't let her stop because I loved the song so much. It was my favourite.

I never knew the name of the lady who took my hand. I just

liked her and loved to be in her company. She taught me to sing the song on our numerous little outings together. I was around three at the time or maybe slightly older. Whenever I heard it over the years, I immediately thought of her and those happy moments walking through the woods. She was probably one of the nurses who worked in the white painted house, Pitfodels Residential Nursery in Aberdeen, where I was first taken into care after recovering in hospital. She wore a matching black trench coat and neat little hat which must have been part of the uniform. Not long afterwards, Pitfodels changed and was renamed Airyhall Children's Home. I never saw the lady again.

Even although I was always blessed with an excellent memory, only small snippets still stand out clearly. One in particular has never left me, yet it happened over fifty years ago. It was the day I met a sulky looking little boy with bright ginger hair. He was being dragged by the hand towards me while I was playing alone in the garden. I didn't pay too much attention at first.

"Patricia!" said a tall slim dark-haired woman. "Do you know who this is?"

I looked at the boy and he glowered back at me. There was no trace of a smile anywhere on his face. Even I could tell he didn't want to be here. It was very plain.

"No," I replied, in a disinterested matter-of-fact voice.

"This is your brother Billy."

I suppose the woman wondered why there was so little reaction from me. Maybe she was disappointed. Her words meant nothing simply because I didn't know what a brother was. I was more interested in pedalling my bike. Perhaps my brother Billy watched me as I took off at breakneck speed towards the orchard, which marked the limits of the garden. When I glanced back for a second, he and the woman were gone and that was that. I never thought any more about it. A couple of months later I would meet him again, when I was transferred to Rose Hill Children's Home.

⌘

I was too old to stay at Airyhall but much too young to know where I was going. All I knew was it was now time to leave my little room. This was my first time going outside in the dark. I felt quite excited. A tall lady with black hair and wearing a tightly fitting tweed coat introduced herself as Mrs Robertson. She led me to the black car parked all by itself in the driveway. I noticed the loud crunching sound made by the gravel under my feet. Everything sounded so different in the dark. I felt cold. After placing a small cardboard suitcase in the boot, Mrs Robertson opened the front passenger door. I recognised the familiar smell of polish as soon as I climbed in and made myself comfortable on the leather seat.

The night was wild and windy. We drove through the darkness of the countryside without saying a single a word. There was nothing much to see either, but I felt warm and comfortable and sleepy listening to the hum of the engine rising and falling. The light of the speedometer on the dashboard kept drawing my attention. It looked like a clock and I watched fascinated as the large needle in the centre moved round and back, round and back, over and over again. It didn't do much else, so after a while, I became bored looking at it.

The car headlamps pierced the inky blackness ahead and transformed the tall trees on either side of the road into pointing spindly fingers and frightening ghastly faces. Suddenly, I felt a slight bump underneath the car. I lurched forward sharply. Mrs Robertson cried out. My head slammed into the dashboard. Pain. Tears. Confusion. I screamed out in the darkness. The car came to an abrupt stop.

"You're all right, you're OK," shouted Mrs Robertson, repeating the words several times until I finally understood them. I was safe. Her hand pulled my head backwards and fingers pinched my nose to stem the flow of blood and calming words brought further reassurance.

"Hold your nose," she said after a minute or so had passed. "Pinch it like this." She pinched her own nose to demonstrate the action so I would understand. "It will stop," she said in a firm but gentle voice.

I held my nose tightly between my fingers. Mrs Robertson got out of the car to check for any damage. When she got back in again, she handed me a handkerchief to cover my nose. The bleeding had almost stopped. She turned the car around and we drove back to Airyhall.

I was quickly taken out the car and up the large winding staircase to my old room and put straight to bed. I left Mrs Robertson standing in the hall entrance way trying hard to explain what had happened. I fell asleep almost immediately but awoke the next morning with a splitting headache. The pain was excruciating. I screamed and cried out until a doctor arrived.

The doctor was young and had a gentle soothing voice and a friendly smile which instantly put me at ease. The pain started to go. He examined me and concluded there was little to worry about. I was probably still suffering a little bit from the shock of the accident and the stress of the move, nothing more. Then he put a hand in his pocket and produced a shiny new penny and told me to watch carefully. The penny danced across his fingers and disappeared and reappeared again. I was fascinated and laughed aloud. My eyes followed the penny's every movement. By the time the doctor left, the throbbing pain in my head had almost gone and I was now the proud owner of the magic penny. But, try as I might, I couldn't make the penny dance or disappear across my fingers.

Eventually, I lost interest and fell asleep. When I woke up, the magic penny was nowhere to be seen.

Within a couple of days, I was as bright as a button and fully recovered from the ordeal. Mrs Robertson returned soon after and we resumed the interrupted journey to Rose Hill Children's Home. This time, we set off in the afternoon and arrived there without a hitch.

I always thought the name Rose Hill should conjure up picture-perfect images of lazy summer afternoons, of beautiful gardens and green lawns, of children laughing without a care in the world. But it never did for me. Instead, it meant grey steel gates and railings with spikes on top. They were always cold to the touch and unyielding, never shrinking in size. Their only purpose was to keep me in and the world out. Rose Hill was a place empty of love or words of kindness, where potential was willfully neglected, stifled or just ignored. I grew up believing I was stupid because I was told I was, every day, for years on end. What hopes and dreams and aspirations I ever had, which might have blossomed with a few simple words of support and encouragement and kindness, were dashed by constant insults and words of contempt.

It was a home filled with children whose eyes never laughed. Tragedy had touched each and every one of them. Most had lost their mothers. Some even saw their mums commit suicide. In this place of sanctuary, where there were no cuddles or soothing words of comfort to be found, every child was simply left to get on with life and tragedy and sadness as best they could. In all my years growing up there, I never heard any child talk about ever having a mother.

Rose Hill was a home with two faces. One face was harsh, cold and indifferent, often hidden and secretive. The other was a shell, a sham, a pretence, which only charitable visitors saw served up with tea and fairy cakes. These regular occasions were stage managed, choreographed, designed to show off a happy, caring, wholesome family environment. Well practised party songs were always sung at just the right moment to wring out every last ounce of sympathy. Including "Nobody's Child" was certain not only to tug at the heart strings but also to loosen the purse strings. Yet these occasions also provided the only opportunity for children starved of attention and affection to be noticed and praised.

As far as I was concerned, Rose Hill meant bitterness, not idyllic images. For many years, long after I walked out through its gates for the very last time, I suffered the same nightmare. Night after night, I screamed and pleaded to be let out. My hands gripped tightly on the iron railings. I shook them as hard as I could. They wouldn't budge. No one heard me. Nobody came. I couldn't escape. Usually I wakened up at this point, always in a cold sweat, my heart racing until I regained my senses and realised it was just my nightmare again.

❦

My first hour in the home set the tone for all my years there. One minute I was an infant and the next a child. Care was rigid. There was no gentle transition from one to the other. Within minutes of arriving, I would learn the first of many lessons from my new house mother. She ran the home with a set of unwritten rules in her head. To know what they were meant having to break them, unless you were a mind reader. I wasn't, so I took the punishments and learned quickly. It was the same for most of the children at Rose Hill.

Mrs Robertson and my house mother were too busy chatting to notice me wandering away from their side. Boredom and curiosity had set in. The heavy green door a few steps along the hallway was too much of a temptation. I wanted to know what lay behind it. So

I tiptoed over and gently turned the bright brass door handle. The door opened easily and I peeked in. Shadows flickered across chocolate-brown painted walls. I couldn't see very far inside but I knew it was a kitchen and it was empty. There was nobody about. I stepped through into the creepy atmosphere only to turn around sharply as the door closed behind me with a long drawn-out groan. The kitchen felt warm.

My curiosity of a few seconds ago was all but gone now, replaced by a slight nervousness. I moved quickly towards the centre of the kitchen, past a large square wooden table almost white with years of scrubbing. Tucked neatly underneath were four high backed chairs. They were much taller than me. My gaze searched out the shadows and dark corners and settled on the flames dancing and leaping behind the small window of an old Victorian black-leaded stove tucked into an alcove a few feet away. A large black kettle was whistling quietly on the hotplate. Steam gently played across the alcove's cracked blue and white patterned tiles.

Gradually, I began to see more and more of the kitchen as my eyes grew accustomed to the half darkness. To the left, a wooden door with large decorated panels stood slightly ajar. To the right of the alcove was the tall narrow frame of a wooden window, the lower half partially hidden by the solid outline of a white stone sink. The door had no handle, which was why it was left open. I reached out and curled my small fingers around its sharp jagged edges and pulled hard. The door barely moved. The bottom edge just scraped along the stone floor and stopped. But my will was strong. I was determined to prise it open. With a final tug, the door suddenly lurched towards me to reveal the inside of a large pantry.

I was pleased as punch. High up on wooden shelves stood rows of jelly jam jars filled with homemade raspberry jam. The jam looked delicious, tempting, but the jars were well out of reach. I desperately wanted a taste. The more I looked at the jam the hungrier I felt. I hadn't eaten anything since leaving Airyhall.

I pondered for a moment, wondering how I could get up to the shelves. Then I remembered the chairs underneath the table. I began dragging the nearest one towards the pantry door. The chair was very heavy and awkward to move. I realised it was going to be a difficult task. But I was starving and the raspberry jam beckoned. It took some time to finally manoeuvre the chair into the correct position. I clambered up and balanced on tiptoes and stretched out my fingers as far as they could go. It was enough. My fingers touched smooth cold glass. Very gently, I eased the jar over towards me and down it came. It was now firmly in my grasp. The jar was mine.

Without wasting a further precious second, I ripped off the paper lid and scooped out handfuls of sticky jam straight into my mouth. It tasted delicious. I was too busy enjoying myself to care about the state I was in. I was covered in jam. It was all over my face and hands and in my hair and on my jumper. I was a mess. The kitchen door suddenly flew open.

"You little thief. What do you think you're doing!"

I jumped with fright and almost tumbled from the chair. My hand was still in the jar as I bowed my head in shame. I was guilty, caught red handed. Instinctively, I knew the sharp angry voice belonged to my new house mother. I turned to face the monster. Her eyes glared at me and pinned me to the spot. I couldn't move. I was terrified. She grabbed me by the ears and hauled me off the chair. I cried out in pain.

"I'll teach you to never take anything out of that cupboard again," she shrieked.

My feet barely touched the floor. She dragged me over to the sink and turned on the tap. The water felt ice cold. I howled and screamed and squirmed while she scrubbed and scraped and tugged at my face until satisfied I had learned my lesson. I would never forget it. Many years passed before I set foot in the pantry again.

๑๒

There were eighteen children sitting either side of a long wooden table. I was the youngest. I was also the smallest. We all sat in complete silence. Two large white bowls stood in the centre of the table. One was filled with hot porridge and the other with milk. They were placed there by the house mother just before she led us single file into the dining room.

I was a little apprehensive, not knowing quite what to expect or how to behave. So I copied everyone else and sat as still as a statue, my arms at my side. The other children kept throwing me quick glances out the corner of their eyes. I tried hard not to look at them. But I was a stranger in their midst, an object of curiosity.

Steam rose slowly from the old cracked porridge bowl in a lazy curling motion. I followed it upwards until I found myself gazing at a picture of Jesus hanging on the wall facing me. He was holding hands with lots of children from all over the world. There were red and yellow children, brown and black children as well as white. They all crowded round Him in a big circle. Some of the small children gazed into His eyes. Their faces beamed with love and He smiled gently back at them.

The loud click of the dining room door closing brought me back down to earth. The house mother's looming presence, demanding perfect discipline, no longer hovered over us. Where a moment ago there was order, now only chaos reigned. A cacophony of cries and screams replaced the silence. Little angels changed into snarling animals. Fingers nipped and nails scratched. Elbows dug deep into unprotected sides in a desperate bid to grab the lion's share of the porridge.

Other children fought hard for the milk bowl which disappeared under a mass of greedy grasping hands. I couldn't take my eyes off the girl with the red ginger hair. She shoved and pushed the hardest and screamed the loudest until the heavy bowl lay cradled protectively in her arms. No one could get it now. She let out a wild howl of triumph.

The girl slowly lifted the bowl to her lips and gathered a mouthful of milk in the back of her throat and gargled loudly. All eyes turned to watch in awe. The dining room fell silent. Through gaps in her front teeth, two perfectly formed squirts of milk arced through the air, almost in slow motion. They landed with a plop and a splat, bang in the centre of the bowl. A cheer went up. Her fist punched the air in delight. I felt disgusted. I couldn't face eating any breakfast now.

Small blue plastic breakfast bowls dived in to scoop out the contents of the porridge bowl. Within moments, it was almost empty. I looked up and down the table which now resembled the aftermath of a battle. Blobs of porridge and milk shaped like little islands lay splattered all over its surface. The noise got louder and louder as children shouted and screamed at each other and argued to the point of blows over nothing in particular.

The dining room door opened with a sharp click and the noise stopped abruptly. Children sat bolt upright in their chairs once more as if some switch had been suddenly pressed somewhere. You could have heard a pin drop. Jesus smiled. We all filed out of the dining room as quietly as we entered it, led by the house mother who never said a word. My first breakfast at Rose Hill was over. Within a day or so, hunger overcame my disgust. Weeks later, someone happened to mention the girl with the red ginger hair was my sister, Mary Anne.

Chapter Three

IT WAS AUTUMN and the leaves on the trees outside the home were turning from green to deep red and gold. If it wasn't raining, I was sent outside to play in the playground for hours on end, until the rest of the children returned home from school. The days felt long and they were getting colder.

By now, I was used to the morning routine: the 7 o'clock rise for breakfast, the blue plastic bowl sitting on the table, the piece of cold toast lying on a small white plate at the side, the lumpy porridge. It never varied. I quickly learned just how valuable the slice of toast was. Toast was currency. You could swap it for a toy. Or it could be used to stop someone reporting you to the house mother. Such bargains were struck in whispers and sign language. If you were fortunate enough to find a thick heely on your plate instead of the usual thin slice of buttered toast, your bargaining power increased many times over. The heely, the end slice of a loaf of bread, was prized by every kid. But it was the luck of the draw whose plate it landed on.

The smell of urine was overpowering. It always came from the same dozen beds. Every morning, without fail, they were soaking wet. The stench filled the bedrooms and the hallway and drifted down the stairs to the dining room. It clung to the school uniforms of the children sitting around the breakfast table. But no one mentioned the smell. It was part of the routine, just like the lumpy porridge.

After breakfast, the children piled through to the cloakroom to put on the shiny shoes they spent hours cleaning and polishing the night before. Coats were pulled off pegs and quickly donned and then it was single file past the staff member standing at the back door. After a quick comb of the hair, each child was hustled out the door and on their way to school.

Very occasionally, attempts were made to adopt a child from the home. There was nothing subtle about the process, no preparation, no planning involved. Towards the end of 1959, a lady wearing a tightly fitting tartan skirt and brown jumper suddenly appeared at Rose Hill one Saturday afternoon. She looked very prim and proper. Her face was small and thin. The black horn-rimmed glasses balanced on the bridge of her nose were far too big for her face. Nobody told me her name or that she wanted to adopt me.

One moment I was in the home, surrounded by familiar faces. A short time later I was sitting in her comfortably furnished house. It was somewhere in a well-off area of Aberdeen. I was playing in front of a warm fire. The silence was broken only by the sharp crackling sound of burning coal. Flames sputtered and danced in the hearth. Now and again, tiny fragments of coal shot out the fire and bounced against the metal fireguard. The lady watched me, intently. Her husband sat quietly in the corner.

She suddenly produced a doll and gave it to me. It was the first doll I had ever had and I was delighted. I touched the doll's perfect face and explored underneath the green matinée jacket and woollen leggings. The lady seemed pleased by my reaction. A smile crossed her face.

"What name would you like to call her?" she asked.

A name popped into my head. "Susan," I replied.

The doll became my baby. I cradled her in my arms and told her off for being naughty. "Naughty Susan. You're a bad baby," I said, over and over.

As I sat on the living room carpet, lost in an imaginary world, the back of my head felt itchy. I scratched it. My hair felt warm from the heat of the fire. The lady stopped smiling. She stared at me, wide eyed, panic written all over her face. Then she moved behind me, slowly, deliberately, and lifted a strand of hair on my head. Her jaw dropped. She let out a shrill shriek.

"She's crawling!"

The strand of hair slipped from her fingers. She stumbled backwards, as if unable to comprehend the enormity of what she'd just seen. But they were there, lots of them, small obscene little creatures, growing more grotesque and threatening with every passing second. The lady wiped her fingers on her skirt, then turned around in small tight circles, flapping her arms, not knowing what to do next.

"You filthy dirty kid!" she hissed. She was angry at me and I didn't understand why. I pulled away, trying to smile sweetly. The doll fell from my hand, never to be picked up again. The lady turned on her startled husband and screamed out.

"Get her coat on. She's going back!"

He meekly obeyed and grabbed my arm roughly and slipped on my coat. Seconds later, I was out the house and in the car. Within the hour, I was back at the home again and put straight into bed. When I awoke the next morning, my white pillowcase was crawling with head lice. Of course, I didn't realise what they were. To me, they were just some new playmates, to prod and poke and have fun with. I begged the staff not to take them away. Later on that day, my long wavy hair was cut to within an inch of my scalp.

Over the years, I've often wondered about the lady and the life I might have had. She was looking for perfection. Instead, she found imperfection, damaged goods. I realised I was simply a doll, just like Susan. The lady never returned to the home.

I told George all about her. How I loved talking to George. He was the only one who listened to me and he didn't make fun of my short hair either. Whenever I needed him, he was always there for me, without fail. He never scolded me. He was never angry. He was my best friend which made me feel good inside. I loved his smart soldier's uniform covered in lots of medals.

It was nearly lunchtime. I could tell by the strong smell of boiled cabbage wafting through the home. It soaked into the nooks and crannies of every room and corridor. There was no escaping the pungent smell. I also knew it was lunchtime by the muffled sounds of pots and pans clattering in the kitchen. The sounds were welcome. I hated the heavy silence when all the children were away at school. The home seemed so empty without them. I longed to go to school but I was still too young.

I suppose that's why I enjoyed being in George's company, in the committee room, at lunchtimes. He never looked upon me as a nuisance. He listened as I related in detail all the bad things I was going through. I told him everything, about all the times I was smacked or when someone was unkind to me or even when I was happy. But I didn't feel that way very often. George was old and wise. His eyes always smiled as he looked down at me, patiently listening to all my long tales of woe. The committee room was in the private and more comfortable part of the home. It was always unlocked in the middle of the day. That was why I was able to sneak in and talk to George for a little while on my own. I sat down at the large table in the centre of the room waiting for the house mother to appear.

She arrived moments later. Luckily for me, she always assumed I'd been in the room for no more than a minute or so ahead of her.

To be found in there without the house mother's permission meant a telling off at the very least, or much worse if she was in a bad mood. Although I knew the room was out of bounds to all children, I was prepared to take the risk if it meant I could talk to George. She never discovered my secret.

An old lady dressed in scruffy clothes always joined us for lunch. But she never ate anything, only watched. I loved it when the sun shone through the tall bay windows, warming the highly polished table. The committee room was sparsley furnished, with an old black fireplace built into the centre of the wall at the far end. An old-fashioned mahogany chest of drawers stood against an adjacent wall. I loved to walk around the large room, smelling the freshness and polish and admiring the many paintings hanging on the walls.

A bowl of hot soup was placed in front of me. It was the same evey day. The house mother stirred the soup and broke a slice of bread into tiny pieces. Then she placed the pieces of bread in the bowl. I watched them swimming around in circles on the surface of the soup.

"Look at the fishies!" she always said.

I was all but invisible after that, neither heard nor seen, even by the staff who popped in from time to time to serve up the rest of the meal. Perhaps it was because I was so small, sitting on the high-backed chair with my head barely peeking above the table's edge. I was easily missed. I was unimportant. But I didn't mind. All I could think about was the school playground a short distance away, from where the sounds of children playing drifted in and out of the room. As I turned my head towards the joyful sound, looking out the window and across the garden filled with roses of all different colours, I just longed to be there with them, to escape into their world of happiness. When the school bell rang and the playground emptied and the sounds faded and died away to nothing, our lunch was over, too. The house mother and her friend never saw me give George a little smile as I quietly left the room.

George White listened but never said a word because he couldn't. He was a painting hanging on the wall. Although he lived and died many years before I was born, somehow I felt connected to him, perhaps because we shared the same surname. So he filled the emptiness I felt at the time. With his silvery grey hair and dressed in his bright red uniform, George brought a little comfort to a lonely child crying out for love in a world which made little sense. A few months later, I was old enough to go to school. I couldn't sneak into the committee room any more. George, like all old soldiers, gradually faded away. But he was never forgotten.

Many years later, I asked my brother Billy about the old lady. He couldn't remember any old lady ever being at the home at the time. I was really puzzled by this. Then a letter arrived from my sister Mary Anne with an old family photograph inside. I stared at the fading image in disbelief. Standing in the photograph was the old lady from the committee room, my gran, who died before I was born.

Suddenly it all made sense. Thinking back, I never actually saw her enter the committee room. I assumed she did, simply because she was there. Now I understood why she never talked or ate anything. She couldn't. She was a spirit, a ghost, who appeared day after day to watch over me. The house mother never saw her. I was the only one who did.

❦

June and I were the youngest in the home, so we were the first to be sent to bed. We shared the attic room, the little girls' room as it was always called. Usually, four children slept in there. But, with only the two of us sharing, we had plenty of room. I hated going to bed early when the evening sun shone. When I heard the sounds of children laughing and playing in the run-down allotments on the other side of the wall, it felt more like a punishment. The children lived in the houses surrounding the home. I watched them from my bedroom window dressed in my pyjamas. They played and ran across the field, through weeds where strawberries and all kinds of vegetables once grew. I longed to be down there with them, to feel their happiness and freedom.

Sometimes, I almost expected to see the old man in the black baggy jacket and bonnet leading his lovely big Clydesdale horse along the narrow path separating the allotment plots from the wall of the home. I used to wait for him every day, after the rest of the children came home from school. One of the older girls had to stay with me because I was too young to be out there on my own.

Soon, I heard a faint clippity clop in the distance. It was the sound I was waiting for. Horse and master were slowly making their way through the field at the back of the allotments. Nearer and nearer they came, past a hotchpotch of wooden sheds and corrugated iron shelters used for all sorts of gardening tasks. My excitement grew to bursting point until they finally came into full view.

"Please, mister, can I have a ride on your horse?" I said, as soon as the old man was within hearing distance. "Go on, mister, let me ride your horse," I pleaded.

The old man said nothing as he passed me by. I tried once more, summoning up all my powers of persuasion as I followed him, tugging at his jacket sleeve in a final desperate bid to get his attention.

"Just a wee ride, mister!" I cried out, and turning around with a big sigh, the old man smiled grudgingly, before giving in as we both knew he would. It was a daily ritual.

"Up you get, lass. Just a wee ride then," he would say. "Hold on tight."

I grabbed the horse's reins and proudly sat on its broad back as the old man led us along the path until we reached the main road. The distance was no more than 100 yards. The horse stopped and the old man helped me down and I made my way back to the home happy and delighted. I loved riding on the horse. Then one day, I waited at the side of the path as usual and they never came. Next day, I did the same, listening hard for the faint clippity clop. I waited every day for a week or more. But I never saw the old man or the horse again.

The sound of squeaking bed springs snapped me out of my sadness. I turned around. June was bouncing on her bed, laughing and leaping in the air out of pure joy. I couldn't resist joining her. What fun, trying to see who could jump the highest.

I don't know how I managed to miss the mattress. But I did, and crashed to the floor in a heap. I was winded slightly but unhurt. I looked at June and she looked at me and we burst into a fit of giggles. June carried on jumping while I climbed on top of the pink chest of drawers next to the window. I wanted get a better view out over the fields. The last rays of sunshine were streaming into the bedroom. Outside, I could still hear the sounds of several lone voices coming from somewhere within the gathering gloom. As I sat balanced on my knees on the dresser, trying to find a more comfortable position, I accidentally brushed a small porcelain trinket pot. It fell to the floor with a crash and shattered into tiny pieces.

I gasped out in horror and glanced over to June who was standing stock still on her bed. She stared back at me with mouth wide open. There was only silence. The enormity of the situation was slowly dawning on us both. We were in trouble. Feverishly, we picked up the fragments now lying scattered on the wooden floorboards and placed them gently on my bed.

"What are we going to do now?" asked June, in a nervous faltering voice which almost bordered on blind panic.

"I don't know, I don't know," I said.

I hardly noticed I was automatically trying to fit the tiny pieces back together again. Perhaps I was desperately hoping they would all magically stick themselves together. But I knew in my heart they wouldn't. We were fast running out of ideas and terrified of what was going to happen to us if the house mother found out. We thought of hiding the pieces under our beds but decided that would be no good. The pieces were sure to be discovered when the staff came in to make the beds in the morning.

"What about the drawers?" I suggested.

But we quickly discarded that idea, too, after June reminded me clean clothes were always put in the drawers once a week. So the pieces were bound to be discovered sooner or later. We would have to think of something fast. Time was running out. Then it struck me. Why not throw the pieces over the wall and into the field? It was overgrown. No one would find them there. June grinned and I smiled back at her. It was a great idea.

I clambered up onto the pink chest of drawers again and tugged and pulled at the top half of the wooden window frame. At first, it refused to budge an inch. I tugged all the harder. My face turned bright red and the muscles in my arms ached with the strain. Finally, it slid down just far enough for me to get a clear shot over the wall and into the field. We both let out a huge sigh of relief.

I jumped down and gathered all the broken pieces together. It was much tougher to climb back up this time using just the one hand. But when you're desperate, all things are possible. I manoevered myself as near to the open window as I dared and pulled my arm right back. I wanted to put as much force into the throw as I could. We both held our breath for a second. June crossed her fingers tightly. Then I launched the pieces out into the half darkness for all I was worth.

Almost immediately, we heard the tinkling sounds of the porcelain fragments bouncing off the stone step underneath the window. I looked down and a head popped out from far below me. My heart sank as I recognised the face glaring up at me. It was the house mother. Now she knew. The evidence was there for her to see. I scrambled off the dressing table and flew into bed. June was already underneath the covers, doing the only sensible thing you can do under such dire circumstances, pretending to be asleep, denying to the world she had anything to do with it.

So that left only me to face the music. I listened in terror as each passing moment brought the house mother's angry footsteps closer and closer. I followed them across the sitting room floor then onwards and upwards as she climbed the stairs until she was within inches of the bedroom door. My grip tightened instinctively on my pyjama bottoms. I cringed and shrank further into the bed covers hoping she wouldn't find me. But it was no use. I knew only too well what was coming. The door flew open and she howled out in rage.

She grabbed me. I tried to wriggle out of her grasp, but her grip was far too strong. The bed covers flew off. Down came my pyjama bottoms. I felt a sharp stinging pain and tears filled my eyes. She screamed at me but I didn't hear the words as more sharp stabs of pain followed.

"I'm sorry, I'm sorry, I won't do it again!" I cried out.

But the pain continued and June still pretended to be fast asleep. The house mother yelled at me again but she wasn't smacking me anymore.

"You get down to the big boys' room. You'll sleep in there tonight!" she ordered.

Still sobbing, I pulled up my pyjama bottoms and slowly made my way along the corridor and down the long staircase, hanging on to the wooden banister for support. Never having been inside the big boys' room before, I didn't know what to expect. I timidly turned the bedroom door handle and went in.

Apprehension instantly turned to delight on seeing my brother Billy. He was standing beside his bed getting changed. There were other boys in the room, too, all older than him. But I hardly noticed them. The only person I saw was my brother Billy. Nothing else mattered, not even the house mother's angry words or the pain of the last few minutes or the fact I was in the big boys' room as a punishment. The single bed in the corner of the room caught my attention. It was covered by a woven bedspread. The bed was empty.

"Is that my bed Billy?" I asked.

At first, I only vaguely registered the silence in the room. I moved halfway towards the bed, then stopped. No one was talking. Nobody was getting ready for bed. All the boys were standing still, staring hard at me. They made me feel uncomfortable, uneasy, unwanted. The atmosphere felt tense, almost hostile, and I was frightened.

Billy sensed the change in atmosphere, too. Without warning, some of the boys moved slowly towards me. They had a look on them I never saw before. I knew them all, but now I wanted to run away from them. I didn't understand what was happening. Suddenly, Billy jumped in front of me, shielding me, shouting at them angrily. The boys backed off. The tension in the air melted away. I felt relaxed. But when I tried to get into bed, Billy pulled me back.

"You're not sleeping in there. You're sleeping in my bed tonight," he said.

I didn't object. I was over the moon at the thought of cuddling into my big brother. He made me feel safe. I couldn't stop talking either. I had a million and one questions inside me, all bursting to get out. Poor Billy.

"Why is the grass green, Billy?" I asked, barely pausing for breath or to listen to his answer.

"It just is," he replied. "Just get to sleep."

"Billy, is Johnny your best friend? Do you like me better, Billy? Why do you like Johnny?"

"Shut up and get to sleep!"

Another question followed, and another and I nudged and poked him each time for the answer. He got more and more annoyed as the long night dragged slowly by. Eventually, he fell fast asleep. I don't know whether it was out of pure exhaustion or me finally running out of questions. As I lay in darkness and the silence of the unfamiliar room, I thought only about the house mother and what she did to me. How I hated her even more now. I felt hurt and angry and wished more than anything else she would die.

When I awoke the next morning, I wasn't thinking about my sore bottom any more. All I could think of was breakfast. At first, I didn't really notice how quiet the home was. I did think it odd there was no house mother to lead us into the dining room as usual. Some of the older children acted strangely. There was none of the normal shouting and screaming. They talked together in small huddles, whispering amongst themselves. Then I heard them mention the house mother and how she was found dead in her bedroom upstairs.

Although I felt very sad, I didn't fully understand I would never see her again. It only began to sink in when there were no more fishies in the committee room, or outings to Nigg Bay, where once June and I covered ourselves in the bright red lipstick we took from her handbag. She was really angry on that occasion, too.

As the years passed, the sadness grew because we parted under such a dark cloud. Good or bad, she was the only mum I ever knew. In the days and months following her death, no one thought to ask me how I was feeling. No one cared enough to see whether or not I was coping. I was just left to get on with it.

Inside me, I also carried the guilt of wishing her dead. For years, I really thought I was responsible. When Billy told me he saw her ghost one night while raiding the pantry, I was too terrified to go down the stairs to the toilet on my own in the dark. So I wriggled about in agony until I wet the bed.

Chapter Four

SHE INTRIGUED ME the moment I saw her. I was playing outside in the playground at the time. The smartly dressed lady walked purposefully up the driveway to the front door of the home. With a green jacket nipped in at the waist and a matching pencil skirt and feather boa hat, she looked the picture of elegance. In her right hand, she carried a small black handbag, matching the colour of her high-heeled shoes.

After ringing the doorbell and waiting a moment, the lady went inside. A few minutes later, she came out and walked back down the driveway with Thomas in tow, one of the young boys from the home. Later, they returned to the home in time for tea. For the next few weeks, the lady came back every Sunday, taking Thomas out for the afternoon each time.

One Sunday afternoon, she didn't turn up as usual. Next day, I was surprised to see her sitting in the dining room. After watching us all take our places at the breakfast table, she stood up.

"Be quiet!" she snapped.

An expectant hush fell over the dining room. All eyes turned towards her.

"Children, I have an announcement to make."

She paused, deliberately, waiting for complete silence. Her eyes darted back and forth, from face to face, fixing every eye for an instant with a steely gaze. Satisfied she now had our undivided attention, she cleared her throat slightly.

"I am your new house mother. Carry on with your breakfast."

The announcement was short and to the point. Without uttering another word, she hurredly left the dining room. If none of us knew quite what to make of her, she wasted no time in showing us. When Thomas said something which annoyed her, she threw him into a small dark cupboard and leaned back smiling with her full weight against the door. He banged and pushed and screamed to be let out. We all watched in disbelief. Now we knew what our new house mother was like and what would happen to us if we stepped out of line.

⌖

During the early fifties and sixties, it was fashionable for many local organisations to hold Christmas parties and invite children along from all the children's homes. One such event was organised by the WRI (Scottish Women's Rural Institutes). We dressed up in our best second-hand party clothes and walked to the hall, arriving just before 3 o'clock in the afternoon when the party was due to start.

As I entered the hall, it wasn't the Christmas tree at the far end which caught my attention, although tall and beautiful and highly decorated. No, it was the long table on which lay dozens of large plates piled high with cakes of every concievable colour, size and shape. There were chocolate cakes, cream cakes, pink dainty cakes, and cakes full of delicious, oozing jam. What an assortment. I never saw so many goodies in my life all in one place. I couldn't take my eyes off them.

The children were running about shouting and screaming and

letting off steam. The noise was almost ear splitting. But I didn't join them because I was more interested in the cakes sitting temptingly on the long table. The table was hidden by a white tablecloth reaching almost to the floor. There were chairs neatly tucked around it, all ready and waiting for the hungry hordes. I slowly walked along the length of the table eyeing up each pile for a second or so, trying to make up my mind where the best cakes were so I could sit within easy reach of them. I didn't want any other kid taking the cakes I wanted. The trouble was they all looked so delicious and I didn't know which ones to choose. My mind was in a bit of a turmoil. It was a hard decision to have to make and time was fast running out.

I grabbed the nearest cake from a plate and dived out of sight underneath the table cloth. Being so small, no one noticed me. I took a sample bite and then carefully placed the cake back on the pile underneath another cake so the bitemark wouldn't be seen. I repeated the whole sneaky process again and again and by the time I reached the bottom of the table, the ducking and diving underneath had become a well practised routine. Finally, I felt satisfied, after tasting every cake. Now I knew which ones I was going to have.

Just then I heard the children being shouted through to the hall. I quickly sat on a chair to make it appear I was the first to take my place at the table. No one suspected anything. But no sooner had the children tucked into the feast laid out in front of them, an older girl, sitting close by me, let out a wail of disappointment.

"I'm not eating that. It's got a big bite in it!"

As she threw the cake down onto the table, there was another cry from further along.

"This one's got a bite in it, too."

Other children added their voices to the growing clamour as each discovered a bite had been taken out of their chosen cake.

Before I knew it, the place errupted into a small riot. Cakes were being thrown here, there and everywhere across the table. I sat quietly smiling, feeling rather full up, pretending to be a complete innocent. I was having a great party but nobody else was.

The women from the WRI were not amused. They found the chaos extremely difficult to cope with. I don't suppose they ever imagined the afternoon turning out the way it did. Eventually, control was restored with the entry of the jelly and ice cream. But it was a close call.

The plump lady seemed to be one of the main organisers. She kept giving me suspicious looking glances. I'm sure she noticed the amount of chocolate and jam and sticky icing which was plastered all down the front of my party dress. But not being able to prove I was the culprit, there was nothing she could do or say. I was so thrilled at the thought of getting away with it.

However, she remembered me the following year, when the same party was held again in the same hall. Only this time, the lady kept a wary eye on me. She never once let me stray anywhere near the table. And of course, the party passed off perfectly.

Christmas was always a magical time for me. There was an electric charge all around the home. The children became more and more excited as the big day drew near. But before then, there was Mr McDonald's party to look forward to. Apart from Christmas itself, it was always the highlight of the festive season.

On the day of the party, we were all told to go upstairs to dress up in our best clothes. My room overlooked the front garden and the long driveway. So I was first to hear the sounds of the catering vans arriving at the front door. Watching it all from my window, I was transfixed. Van doors were flung open and a procession of waitresses in neat white aprons and caps carried large platters of food smartly into the home. Then they unpacked cuttlery, plates and glasses and laid the table. The sounds generated by this frenzy of activity continued for several more minutes until silence indicated the end of this well-practised drill.

I quickly finished dressing and hurried out my bedroom to join the other children waiting in the playroom downstairs. We were instructed to wait there so we wouldn't get in anyone's way. An hour later, all was ready. We were led through to the dining room, now magically transformed into a banqueting hall. The two long wooden tables, normally bare, were covered in the finest of linen and tableware. Our eyes popped out in amazement.

The house mother was already sitting waiting for us at the small table where she usually sat. It was positioned in between the two long tables so she could easily keep an eye on us all. Although our excitement was just about unbearable, everyone knew better than to let go of their feelings, even on such a day. Her eagle eyes watched closely, missing nothing. As we made our way to our normal sitting positions, no one talked, or whispered, or did anything which might bring her disapproval.

The silence was at last broken by the entrance of the waitresses, expertly carrying plates of sliced turkey, hot steaming roast potatoes and vegetables with lashings of gravy. They moved with clockwork precision, placing a plate neatly in front of every child, but never smiling or uttering a single word. I was served by a waitress who appeared to be slightly older than the others. Eyes and cheeks were plastered with heavy makeup and lips were covered by the brightest red lipstick I ever saw. Her greying hair was dyed black to give a younger look. I was sure her make-up would crack if she smiled.

Such mouth-watering food was devoured without mercy. Not a scrap was left on any plate. The house mother looked pleased. Without an apparent word from anyone, the waitresses returned from the kitchen and cleared the tables ready for the ice cream and jelly. Despite the clatter of plates and the jingle of cutlery, there was still barely a whisper from any of us.

Midway through the ice cream and jelly, Mr McDonald made a grand entrance carrying fistfuls of small brown envelopes. There was a presence about him, an aura which filled the room. Tall and smartly dressed, balding with black square-framed glasses, Mr McDonald looked every inch the successful business-man. He reminded me of Sgt Bilko in the TV comedy programme.

Slowly, he made his way up and down the tables. He paused for a moment at the back of every child. Then he placed an envelope on the empty plate at each child's side before moving on. This was the highlight of the afternoon, expected and much anticipated. For we all knew what was inside the envelope. When he was finished, Mr McDonald turned around and faced the room and wished us all a merry Christmas.

When we had polished off the last traces of the ice cream and jelly on our plates, Mr McDonald left the dining room along with the rest of the staff. The waitresses sprang into action for the last time and rapidly cleared the tables of the remaining plates and cutlery. Finally, they pulled off the tablecloths and transformed the tables once more into their usual wooden bareness.

Throughout this final flurry of activity we remained where we were, sitting calmly waiting for the last waitress to go and the kitchen door to close for the last time. Then all pandemonium broke loose. The silence and solemnity of the afternoon was torn apart. Fingers ripped open envelopes and children squealed with delight holding up a ten bob note in their hand. It was a small fortune. The hubbub of shrill chatter was about only one thing: the toys we were going to buy with the money.

But the excitement was short lived. A suggestion was made later on that the ten bob notes should be handed over for safe keeping.

A member of staff collected the money and the envelopes and they were never to be seen again.

Mr McDonald did a lot for the home over many years, providing not just the party every Christmas, but also free cinema and theatre tickets and much more. He was a kind and caring man who tried to make our lives just a little bit better.

Christmas Eve arrived soon after. The tall tree in the dining room covered in decorations and lights looked even prettier than the day before. With each passing moment, the buzz of anticipation grew louder. By now, the excitement was plainly visible on every child's face. There was only one topic of conversation. What was Santa going to bring?

Bedtime came at last. I ran up the stairs and into the little girls' room which June and I now shared with two more girls, sisters Margaret and Catherine. Eventually, they all fell asleep. But I forced myself to stay awake because I wanted to see Santa. I had to know what he actually looked like. Was he really jolly and kind? Was he scary? If I saw him, should I talk to him or pretend to be sleeping? What if he knew I was pretending? Would I still get my toys? These thoughts and many more filled my mind. All I could think about was Santa as the minutes dragged slowly by. I lay quietly on my bed staring at the stars peeping through the curtainless window facing me. Far-off city noises and the sound of muffled voices from downstairs gently broke the silence in room. I turned over on my side, then back again, both restless and tired at the same time. I tried my hardest to stay awake, but I fell asleep.

When I opened my eyes, it was morning. Sleepily, I lifted my head off the pillow and sat up and looked around. There was a long misshapen pillowcase perched awkwardly at the bottom of my bed. The room was filled with squeals of delight and shouts of "Santa's been! Santa's been!" and then I realised I must have fallen

asleep and missed him. But my disappointment only lasted as long
as it took me to reach the bottom of the bed.

My fumbling fingers searched deep inside the pillowcase and
pulled out a doll. She was dirty. An arm was missing. Half her
blonde hair had fallen out. I was puzzled. My head and arms all but
disappeared as I delved back into the pillow once more. Fingers
searched and probed and closed around a second doll. I pulled her
out into the light for a closer inspection. I decided I didn't like
her either. She was so ugly looking. Her eyes met in the middle of
her nose.

"Ugh. Cockeyed!" I shouted out in disgust. I dropped her
quickly and she tumbled to the floor. My hand reached in again.
This time I brought out books and annuals and a jigsaw puzzle, all
of which I piled next to me on the bed. I took a book from the pile
and opened it, eager to look at the pictures. But every page was
covered in scribbles. Pages were missing. Some were torn. As I
grabbed the jigsaw, pieces spilled out the box and onto the bed. The
box was ripped.

Once more I searched the pillowcase. But now it was empty and
crumpled up in a shapeless heap. There were no more toys left in
it. I felt a little sad. Then my fingers stumbled upon something
small and thin at the very bottom. I pulled it out. It was a letter.
Even though I couldn't read yet, I felt very pleased. No one had
ever sent me a letter before. The letter made me feel very important. I jumped off the bed and opened the attic room door and
rushed down the five wooden steps leading to the the big girls'
room where my sister slept.

"Lottie, Lottie!" I shouted breathlessly, hardly able to get the
words out. "Someone's given me a letter."

"Hmmm," groaned my big sister.

She wasn't fully awake yet. But I forced myself into her bed and
pushed the letter to within an inch of her face.

"Read it, read it!" I shouted.

"Give me a minute," said Lottie, rubbing the sleep from half-opened eyes. She grabbed the letter from me, annoyed by my demanding attitude, and then moved it backwards and forwards slightly in front of her face until the writing came into focus. Then she read it out aloud. It was from a lady who owned a toy shop. She wanted to be my new mummy and I would have lots of different toys to play with every day. I had to write back to her.

My face lit up. Someone wanted to give me lots of new toys. I felt happy but also a little sad because I didn't know how to write back to the lady. Lottie didn't see my sadness. She was now too busy discovering what was inside her own pillowcase. So I returned to my room to play with my broken toys.

After breakfast was over and the plates cleared away, the dining room was filled with the chaotic sounds of excited children. Boys whizzed about noisily all over the place playing with aeroplanes and cars. Girls played quietly with their dolls. In one corner sat my brother Billy, lost in a world of his own. He was playing with the battered shell of a small car. The car had no wheels. But that didn't seem to bother him as he drove it along an imaginary road in the air. We laughed and argued over the jigsaw puzzle he was also given as a present. Even although a dozen pieces were missing, somehow we still managed to finish it.

Despite broken toys and missing jigsaw pieces and scribbled-in books, nothing could take away the magic or the excitement or the enjoyment of Christmas. Broken toys were better than no toys. As for the letter, it simply disappeared. I wondered about it for many years afterwards, trying to figure out who wrote it and who put it in my pillowcase. But it was a mystery without any answers.

⚜

It was early evening and I was having fun in the bath. Edith was showing me how to get the bathwater very soapy and to blow bubbles using my fingers. Everytime I managed to blow a bubble and make it rise into the air I squealed out with delight. We sang the song "I'm Forever Blowing Bubbles" and Edith noticed I was very happy and over excitable.

"What have you been doing today?" she casually asked.

Not realising what I was really saying, I blurted out, "I went to the funfair and went on all the rides with my sister Lottie and my big sister Mary Anne."

"So who had the money to take you on all the lovely rides?" said Edith.

I innocently told her Mary Anne, not wanting to be distracted from blowing more bubbles. I forgot Mary Anne's warning, not to tell anyone where I was today. Without realising it I landed her right in trouble. Mary Anne was later accused of stealing £5 from the house mother's purse. It was a small fortune in the late 1950s.

Of course, I didn't know anything about any money as we made our way to the beach in the early afternoon Easter sunshine. I walked in between Lottie and Mary Anne, holding their hands and chattering non-stop. We were having a great adventure.

We never quite made it to the water's edge and instead found ourselves walking slowly along a small road running parallel to the beach, moving towards the lights and sounds of a distant funfair. As we got nearer, the indistinct buzz in the air swelled up then died on the breeze hitting my face. Gradually, it changed into a wall of sound.

This was my first visit to a funfair. I was dazzled by all the coloured bulbs and flashing lights and deafened by the music blaring out from the carousel and the other rides. For the life of me, I couldn't quite understand how people were screaming out in terror and happy and delighted at the same time. It was all fascinating and a little bit scary at first. My head was spinning around in all directions trying to take in the new and exotic sights and sounds. The delicious smell of burgers and fried onions and candyfloss hung in the air making me hungry. Men in cloth bonnets and ladies wearing headsquares and large gold earrings stood behind wooden stalls, jingling money in their big apron pockets, tempting the passing mums and dads and young teenagers enjoying the Easter holiday to part with their hard-earned wages.

All afternoon they shouted out, voices hoarse and cracking under the strain, trying their best to be heard above the constant whine of nearby generators providing the power for the dozens of rides at Aberdeen's famous Codona's Carnival. Mary Anne tugged at my hand as we weaved through the milling crowds to the high aluminium steps leading onto the waltzers. My sister handed over some money and a heavy bar slammed down to keep us safely in our seats.

We were off a few seconds later, spinning around in one direction and then the other, going faster and faster, until I could no longer move any part of my body. My stomach felt like it was rising up into my mouth and I just wanted the ride to be over. Not so Mary Anne and Lottie, who both enjoyed every second, screaming to the heavens.

The ride stopped and I got off feeling extremely disorientated and rather queasy. I threw up. After that, no amount of coaxing by my sisters would get me back on the waltzers. So they left me to watch them. On they went, again and again, enjoying the thrills. Every time the waltzer stopped, they hopped right back on.

After about the fifth or sixth go, they realized how bored I looked standing at the side, not enjoying myself any more. So we all made our way to the candyfloss stall where the woman there handed me a giant pink candyfloss wrapped around a stick. The sticky sugar stuck to my hair and covered my clothes but melted in my mouth. How I enjoyed the taste of my first candyfloss.

Before I knew it, my legs were tired and my sisters were dragging me away. The adventure was over and we couldn't be late for tea. They warned me not to tell anyone of our visit to the funfair as we rushed back home with such haste my feet barely touched the ground. Mary Anne and Lottie were relieved to find nobody had missed us.

After tea, I was called through for a bath. The dirt and dust of the funfair and the remnants of the candyfloss sticking to my hair soon disappeared in the lather of bubbles and soapy water. I never knew what punishment Mary Anne received, but it would have been severe.

Chapter Five

EDITH WAS SMALL IN HEIGHT with short, wavy honey-blonde hair. She was either in the kitchen, baking with her sleeves rolled up, or washing the dirt away from my face and hands. A very hard-working country girl, Edith was very set in her ways. But she always had a lot of time for me. Nothing was too much trouble. Edith baked me a large sponge cake for my birthday. It was covered with pink icing and there were five candles on top. She took it through to the dining room where all the children sang "Happy Birthday" to me.

It was the morning of my first day at school. Edith tried to dress me but my non-stop chattering and fidgeting made it difficult for her. She looked exasperated as she tried to do the buttons up on my new school cardigan, telling me all the time to be still. But I wasn't listening to a word she was saying. When she finally managed to get me looking all neat and tidy, Edith warned me to put my dukes up and fight if anyone gave me a hard time or picked on me. She curled her hand into a tight fist so I understood.

"Remember what I told you," she said, opening the back door of the cloakroom.

With a quick wave goodbye, I ran and skipped down the main road to the school a short distance away from the home. I walked into the noisy playground where girls played hopscotch or skipping games and boys ran about all over the place chasing their new-found friends. At last, I was a part of it all, no longer sitting in the committee room listening to the happy sounds of children playing.

As I explored the playground, I came across an old empty bike shed. Next to it was the girls' toilet. When I went in, there was a little boy half naked crying his eyes out. His trousers were lying on the floor. An older girl with long brown hair was strutting about wearing his pants on her head. She taunted him and ignored his pleas to give him his pants back. I saw she was enjoying the power she had over him and it made me angry.

"Give him back his pants!" I demanded.

The boy looked at me and stopped crying.

"No!" the girl said. She took the pants from her head and began to swing them through the air in a circle. I couldn't help myself. The anger bubbled over and I remembered to put my dukes up, just like Edith told me to. I flew at the girl and punched her on the nose. She dropped the pants on the stone floor and ran screaming out the toilet door. The boy gave me a smile. He slipped his pants and trousers on and quickly left. I ran all the way back to the home. Edith was surprised to see me and frogmarched me right back again. I made an enemy and a friend on my first morning at school.

Within the first month, I was off school for several weeks with scabies. I hated the daily ritual, drawing the poison out of my skin which was infected with me scratching so much. "Patsy Whyte," said the house mother, slapping another steaming hot bread poultice onto my skin, "if you don't stop scratching, you'll have to wear a mask."

I was covered in scabs from head to foot which itched like crazy. It was torture. The poultices burned my face and made me yelp and jump about in pain. They always felt too hot and I dreaded them. The poultices were applied three times a day. I would rather have worn the mask and asked the house mother when I could get it. But she never meant it and I was disappointed. I thought wearing a mask would be great fun because I could scare the wits out of the other children in the home.

All the while, Edith kept an eye on me as I slowly got back to normal. She was the most important person in my life. By this time, Mary Anne was no longer at the home. One morning, I noticed she was gone. We never said goodbye. I wouldn't see her for another thirty-six years. I didn't have very much to do with my sister Lottie or brother Billy either. We were related, but family ties were never strengthened or encouraged. So they were just like any of the other children at the home. A year or so later, when I was out in the playground, I spotted Lottie through the big steel gates. She was carrying a suitcase and stepping into a big black taxi which drew up outside the home. She never saw me watching her leave. Once more, there was no goodbye. Many years were to pass, too, before I saw her again.

Not long after I went back to school, Edith left the home to get married to a coalman. I saw her standing in the kitchen shortly before her wedding. She was as black as the ace of spades. Her face was covered in soot. She was wearing old sheets made up to look like her wedding dress and paraded on a horse and cart up and down the road outside the home. This was the custom for all brides to be and was supposed to bring them good luck. I was happy for her but also sad to see her go.

Christine took over when Edith left. She was tall and slim and pretty. Aged in her early twenties, Christine's hair was dark and wavy with silver streaks through it. I didn't like her from the word go. She picked on me at every opportunity and sent me to bed straight after tea.

"Bed!" she always said, looking me sternly in the eye while I sat at the table. I dreaded seeing her for I always knew what was coming next. There was no reason to send me to bed for I hadn't done anything wrong. She just didn't like me. This went on for weeks.

One night, I was lying in bed in my room on my own feeling bored and rather fed up. The house mother was in her bedroom next door. She came through unexpectedly and handed me a big bag of marshmallows. There was no explanation. I think she may have felt sorry for me.

Every Tuesday was bath night. It was Christine's job to bathe all the younger children. As I stood outside the bathroom, I overheard her talking to a small boy in the bath.

"I'm going to grab your wee robin. I'm going to get it!" I heard her say.

This was my chance to get rid of the woman who was making my life such a misery. I quietly tiptoed away from the bathroom door, watching where I placed my feet so she wouldn't hear the floorboards creak. Then I ran to the house mother's sitting room. I knew such talk was not tolerated.

The house mother quietly listened at the bathroom door for a minute. Then she threw it open and gave Christine such a dressing down. A fuming row erupted as Christine tried to defend herself. But it was no use. The house mother dismissed her on the spot. I felt a sense of triumph. My life was free of Christine at last. It was all about survival and I was learning fast.

Christine was replaced shortly afterwards by Helen, a kindly quiet middle-aged lady with short black hair. She was very good to me and I liked her very much. She popped into my room on her days off when I was in bed. Every couple of weeks or so, she also gave me a little doll. I don't know who was the happier, me receiving it or Helen giving it to me. The doll was always brand new and still in its box. But I had to keep quiet about it and not tell anyone.

One evening, she told me her mum had died, so she wouldn't be coming to see me any more. I missed her greatly.

Sunday afternoon was always hard for me. The playground was empty so there was no one to talk to or play with. I watched through the bars of the steel gates as fathers arrived at the front door of the home to take their children out for the afternoon. Minutes later, they emerged with their children, all dressed up in their Sunday best. Then they all made their way down the gravel driveway lined with trees and walked out into the freedom I longed for. I watched the same scene unfold every Sunday year after year. The children always looked happy and excited. They were visiting their fathers' houses. So many times I wanted to jump over the gates with their sharp pointed tips and go with them. But I couldn't get out. The gates were padlocked, separating me from their happy world. My eyes followed them as they all filed past. No one ever came for me.

When the children returned, we all sat down for tea. The blue plastic plate in front of me contained two dried-up oatcakes and two slices of bread thinly covered with dried-in jam. Next to them was a small, extremely thin piece of ginger cake, which broke into pieces as soon as it was picked up. A mug of cold tea sat next to my plastic plate. The children were chatty and contented and stuffed full of sweets. Their pockets jingled because they were full of money which was spent at the school tuckshop the following day. I felt jealous and envious.

☙❦❧

The first boy I ever fancied was David who was in my class at school. I was around six and he was slim with light brown hair swept to the side in a parting. But he never noticed me. He was always more interested in playing cowboys and Indians with the other boys.

The playroom at the home was a mess with walls full of holes and bits of broken-off plaster lying scattered across the floor. It was soon to be renovated but in the meantime we all amused ourselves by using small pieces of the plaster as chalk, drawing faces and pictures and graffiti of all kinds on the walls. I remember drawing love hearts but finding a clear space was always the problem. PW L DG, they proclaimed, and there was an arrow drawn right through the middle. It was innocent fun. Naturally, my first crush didn't last very long.

Some years later, when I was playing in the swing park near the home during the summer holidays, I noticed a teenage boy sitting on the swings. I had seen him there before and was starting to get to like him and several times I caught him looking at me. Despite feeling rather shy and awkward, I plucked up the courage to sit on the empty swing next to him and we began talking. He told me his name was James and that he lived in Ferriers, a housing estate of tenement slums not too far away from the swing park. I'd never been there but I knew the reputation it had for poverty and large families and all kinds of squalor. Some of my classmates lived in the estate and always appeared dirty and unkempt.

James asked me where I came from and I pointed upwards, to the home. Because it was perched on top of a hill, it dominated the whole area. From the home's windows, the house mother easily saw the swing park and kept a close watch on everything happening below. It was also a cheap way to keep the children at the home amused and out of the way all day. So we were encouraged to play there.

After I old James my name he paused for a moment or two and then asked me a question which made me cringe inside.

"Is your mother Nanny Whyte?"

I blurted out she was.

James added, in a matter-of-fact voice, "Yeah, I know her. She's a wino. All the kids call her Nanny Wine Paps."

I was stunned and embarrased and if the ground had opened up I would have gladly jumped in to hide the shame. Suddenly, I was the daughter of a wino and everyone knew about it. Why didn't I have the kind of mother everyone else had? My mother was the butt of jokes and sniggers and inuendo. She was looked upon as scum. I felt sick to the stomach. Because I was her daughter, I realised, the outside world would look at me in the same way.

I always tried to hide the fact my mother was an alcoholic from the other children at the home, never bringing her up in any conversation. Once I saw my mother staggering up to the home holding on to my father. It was early evening and I was playing in the playground. She was wearing white high heels and a coat pulled in at the waist and a white headscarf. Her clothes were shabby and dirty and creased, as if she slept in them. I felt embarrassed as they passed by me. My father called out, saying he had a bag of sweets for me. Then they both made their way slowly up the driveway to the front door.

Someone, I don't know who, answered the front door bell and turned them away. I saw it all through the window of the playroom, which I ran into to hide, to feel safe, to be as far away from them as I could. I felt no connection or bond or any sadness either as I watched them disappear down the gravel driveway and out of the home. I just couldn't accept her as my mother. She was not what I always wanted a mother to be and my father was simply a stranger who hung on to her arm, nothing more.

At every opportunity, the house mother liked to remind me who I was and the sort of family I came from. She also took great pleasure in letting me know my future. When I was young, I was a really cute child and the staff at the home and the house mother's eldest daughter liked to take me out with them on Saturday trips to the town to look around the shops. I looked forward to these treats.

If there was someone famous appearing at Her Majesty's

Theatre, and the children from the home were given free tickets, I was always the one dressed in the pretty party frock, scrubbed clean, hair shining, who at the end of the show presented the stars with a bouquet of flowers. Ruby Murray and Andy Stewart were two of the stars I met. But there were many others, all of them well known in the entertainment world at the time. I sat in the audience at the front of the theatre and then up I went when the show ended. Spotlights shone brightly in my face as I looked out into the darkness at the sea of faces in the audience. It was hard to make them out. I smiled sweetly and dropped into a curtsey and then handed over the big bouquet of flowers in my hands. It was almost as tall as I was, neatly tied in a beautiful red silk ribbon. I knew the routine well. I was a real professional.

But the girl with the cute turned-up nose started to grow up and my sweet angelic face changed along with the innocence of a small child. The young girl good enough to present flowers to the stars was now a tink as far as the house mother was concerned. As the years passed, such name-calling became part of everyday life.

I don't exactly know when I first started to feel dirty and unclean inside, or when thoughts of my father and mother started to repulse me, or when I began to loathe and hate them. But over the years, and at every opportunity, the house mother drummed into me how I would turn into an alcoholic, a tink, just like them. By then, my brother Billy and I also lost our Christian names. We were simply referred to as "those Whytes".

"You'll grow up to be a prostitute, just like your mother!" said the house mother venomously, time and time again, always out of earshot of anyone who might be listening. The name-calling, verging on hatred, started to affect me deeply and to drag me down. The other kids at the home started calling me names, too, especially during arguments, when they couldn't get the better of me. Eventually, I started to believe it all and I began to feel more and more unconfortable at school because I thought other people must see me as the house mother did.

One day, in the English class, dark despairing thoughts ran through my head. What was the point of being good at anything? I wasn't going to try any more. So I simply stopped. I didn't think about the lessons any more and never answered questions or put up my hand.

When I was in primary school, I always tried to get the answers right. I really wanted to do well. My ambition then was to become an air hostess and travel the world. I used to lie in my bed and dream about what it must be like to visit foreign countries. But, after years of brainwashing, my life felt bleak and without hope. Any ambitions I may once have had were gone. I sat in class believing I was dirty and not worthy of anything. So I drew more and more into myself with every passing day. I found it increasingly difficult to talk to my classmates, even the ones I knew from years back. They were a mixture of kids, some from very poor backgrounds, who lived in some of the most deprived areas of Aberdeen, and others from better-off families. But I felt nothing in common with any of them. Why would they want to bother with someone like me? My self-esteem was all but gone. I was simply a nothing, a nobody.

For many years, I tried to understand why the house mother subjected me to such cruel mental torture. Why did she once show me off to the world only to turn on me with such venom? Was it something to do with my background, the people and way of life I once represented? I never figured it out. Whatever the reason, her hate-filled words stayed with me, following me like a dark shadow for a very long time.

Chapter Six

EVERYONE WAS TOO BUSY to pay any attention to me, so I sneaked along to the large cubbyhole under the stairs. You were not supposed to go in there but I didn't care. It was my favourite place. Most days I was all but invisible, hardly noticed by members of staff busy with the daily routine, so no one ever missed me.

The cubbyhole was a large cupboard, a private space I made my own. Its shelves were filled with long-forgotten outdated shoes handed into the home over years by well-meaning members of the public. They were cast-offs, gathering dust, mostly adult shoes, which was why I liked trying them on. I slipped on my favourite pair of white stiletto shoes which were far too big for my small feet. But I didn't care. I loved them. I felt all grown up.

One day, I made my way unseen to the cubbyhole as usual and heard muffled voices just as I was about to enter. They were the voices of my brother Billy and sister Lottie. Instead of opening the door and joining them, I pressed my ear against it and listened. They were talking about a ghost that appeared to them one night while in their beds when they lived at Linmoor. The ghost, a lady in grey, swooped through the dormitory past rows of sleeping children, letting out a high-pitched screaming sound as she collected the souls of the dead.

"If she hovered over you and you were awake and caught sight of her black eyes, you'd never wake up again," said Lottie.

Well, hearing that unsettled me, terrified me, and I ran back to the safety of the kitchen. Later, as bedtime approached, I couldn't get the grey lady out of my head. I tried all kinds of excuses and ploys so I could stay up longer. But it was no use.

I lay in bed with my rag doll and old battered teddy bear on either side of me for comfort. Moonlight flooded the room and the rising wind rattled the small attic window. Dark shadows from the branches of the old tree outside in the driveway danced and swayed across the walls. I gripped my bedspread even tighter, convinced the lady in grey was coming and I would be her next victim.

Sleep was all but impossible and morning seemed a long way off. Every few minutes, I plucked up the courage and peeked out from underneath the bed covers. Each time, I half expected the black eyes to be staring back at me. Thankfully, they never did and eventually I drifted off to sleep. My soul was safe for another night.

Linmoor was once an old mansion which was converted into a children's home. It was situated deep in the countryside, surrounded by a forest. Billy and Lottie were there for a short time before they came to the home. Whether it was ever haunted by the ghost of a grey lady, I don't know. More likely, they knew I was listening outside the cubbyhole door that day and wanted to give me a scare. It certainly worked.

⊙✝⊙

I wanted to run around in the playground for a couple of hours more because it was still light outside. But life in the home followed a strict timetable. There were no exceptions to the rules. Still being the youngest, I was always first to go to bed.

Climbing the steps to my attic room, I opened the bedroom door and was surprised to see a young girl sitting in the bed opposite to mine.

"Who are you?" I asked her.

"My name's Josie," she replied.

"You've still got your clothes on. You're supposed to take them off and put your pyjamas on when you go to bed."

But Josie only smiled at me as she fidgeted and bounced about inside the bed covers. I got undressed, put my pyjamas on and sat up in bed looking at her.

Once more, I repeated, "You've not got your pyjamas on."

Josie didn't listen to a word I was saying as her blue eyes darted around the room taking in her new surroundings. I was happy to have a new pal come to stay at the home and I felt we were going to be the best of friends. She was the same age as me, her dark hair cut to just above her neck. And her skin was the clearest I ever saw, pink and glowing, making her look radiant. She was wearing her school uniform.

"When did you come here?" I asked.

"I went to the shops for sweeties. I got murdered," she said, still smiling at me.

I didn't understand what murdered meant as we continued chatting away. All I knew was I liked her and I would be happy tommorrow walking with her to school and being in the same class. I don't remember falling asleep. But when I woke up in the morning, Josie was gone, leaving behind a neat and tidy bed.

I hurried downstairs to breakfast looking for her but she wasn't there. So I asked a member of staff where Josie was.

"She's the new girl," I explained.

"There's no new girl."

"She was in my room last night," I argued back.

The member of staff gave me a strange look and told me to stop

talking and to eat my breakfast so I could get ready for school. I
didn't believe her. I had talked to Josie. She'd talked to me. So she
was bound to be about somewhere. I thought maybe she was
hiding in the home and would turn up ready to go to school with
me. But she never did. I kept looking out for her over the next day
or so. But my new friend was nowhere to be seen. I walked to
school feeling empty inside and sad that we never played together.

Was Josie simply a figment of my imagination? In all my years at
the home, children were never brought in for just one night. The
staff were always aware of any new arrival. We led very sheltered
lives, never watching the news on television or reading any newspapers. I couldn't even read properly. So I never really appreciated
what murdered meant.

I never forgot Josie. Every time I thought about her, a picture of
a happy six-year-old popped into my mind. To me, Josie was real
and solid and very much alive. It was only long after leaving the
home I realised she was not of this world. She was a ghost, a spirit,
someone who brought joy into my life early one summer evening.

Josie wasn't the only friend I made I couldn't quite explain.
There was the young boy Thomas, who used to wait for me every
morning on the way to school. I always saw him standing a little
bit away from the entrance to the home. Then we talked to each
other for a few minutes. He was a rather good-looking boy, aged a
few years older than me with short platinum-blond hair. His hair
fell into a fringe in front of his face. He told me he came from the
run-down flats which were visible running down the nearby brae.

But there was something different about him compared to all
the other schoolkids in the area. He wore a jacket which appeared
much too brightly coloured for the times. I never registered this as
strange until many years later. He also appeared much too clean
and tidy and well dressed for the street he said he lived in. Thomas
stood there, always in the same place, carrying a satchel over his

shoulder. We talked for a few minutes before I said goodbye and continued walking on to school. But I never once saw him leave for school. Whenever I looked back, he was just gone.

When I came back from school, Thomas was waiting for me, standing in the piece of waste ground near the home. He walked with me the few yards to the spot where he stood in the mornings. We said goodbye and I made my way into the home. But I never saw him go into the flats where he said he lived. When I turned around, he was simply not there any more.

These short morning and afternoon meetings went on for some time until one day Thomas announced he was going away. I wouldn't be seing him any more. That made me feel sad. True to his word, one school morning he never turned up. I never saw him standing near the home again.

Many years later, while living in England, I was getting ready to go to work early one morning when there were several loud hard knocks on the front door. My partner John also heard the knocks. We were both in the large hall cupboard putting on our coats at the time. I quickly popped my head out of the cupboard to see who it was and clearly saw a young man standing and smiling on the other side of the large clear window panels making up the front door. He was tall with platinum-blond coloured hair cut into a fringe and wearing a modern brightly coloured padded jacket. I asked John to go and see what he wanted. John poked his head out of the cupboard a second later and said there was no one there.

"But I've just seen him," I said, rather perplexed. "He was standing there clearly."

As I glanced out the front door, all I saw was the empty path leading to the closed gate at the bottom of the garden. There was nobody to be seen. John rushed out into the street and bumped into the postwoman delivering letters. He asked her if she'd seen anyone else in the street in the last few seconds. No, was her reply.

The incident left us both puzzled. All day long, I couldn't shift the nagging feeling that I knew the young man's face from somewhere. Then it clicked. He was the same young man who used to wait for me all those years ago outside the home. His jacket, which once looked so out of place, now fitted in perfectly with the fashion of the 1980s. Coincidence? Mistaken identity? It was yet one more mystery in my life.

❦

When I was a young kid, I totally believed in magic. One evening, shortly before Christmas, we were given free tickets to the theatre to see *Peter Pan*. We had a great time and at the end of the performance we all walked back home.

I wasn't looking forward to this part of the evening for the route home took us past St Nazareth House, a large creepy mansion with grey walls which were once painted white. The black steel gates with gold spear tips on top kept prying eyes out and the nuns and their charges firmly locked inside. The only time I ever saw the St Nazareth kids was on a Sunday, as they walked to church with the nuns. They went to a different church to us and although our paths briefly crossed, they never spoke to you or even smiled. They looked unhappy.

Every week I noticed the same pretty girl with sandy coloured hair. We always exchanged a quick glance at each other, but nothing more. As the years passed, we both watched each other growing up. We were two lonely children on much the same path in life, separated by no more than half a mile. But we were never destined to become the friends I'm sure we would have been if circumstances had been different. Little did we know in a few years time I would be the first girl to switch on the Christmas lights in Aberdeen and the following year, she would be the second.

I met her briefly only once after we both left our homes. She was working at the harbour gutting fish — a freezing job at the best of times but much worse in winter. I was 16 so my social worker got me a job there, too, and during a tea break, I tried to talk to her. I asked her what it was like with the nuns. But she was shy and distant and answered only with a shrug of her shoulders. It was plain she didn't want to speak about the past which had affected her deeply. I knew then the pretty girl who once passed me week after week on the way to church was now no more. The spirit inside her died somewhere along the road.

Although I was tired and ready for bed that evening after the long walk back from the theatre, my mind was still filled with thoughts of *Peter Pan*. I climbed up onto my small pink dressing table underneath the attic window in my room to look at the stars twinkling in the blackness above me. I imagined seeing Peter, Wendy and the Lost Boys soaring through the night sky and longed for them to fly into my bedroom and take me to that magical land called Neverland. Eventually, when tiredness over-took me, I sleepily crawled into my small cosy bed surrounded by old battered toys and cuddled up to my shabby teddies.

I don't know what time it was but it was still dark when I was suddenly awakened by the sound of children laughing and giggling and running all around my bed. As I struggled to focus through half-opened sleepy eyes, I saw a young boy and girl, both about six or seven — the same age as me — dressed in long white gowns. The young girl, who had long black hair with a straight fringe, carried a small teddy and stood at one corner of the bottom of my bed. The young boy, who had short ginger hair, stood at the other corner. They both stared at me, silently, as if suddenly realising I was awake and looking at them. I was not afraid. It all felt quite natural.

I don't know if the words were actually spoken, or if they were somehow transplanted into my mind, but I knew the little girl was asking me if I wanted to play with them. I said, "Yes". Then they both walked up either side of the bed and the little girl touched my head, telling me to take in a deep breath.

The next thing I knew they were supporting me on either arm and I felt I was soaring through the night sky. It was a wonderful feeling. They told me they were taking me to see the Milky Way. I remember flying about and having fun until it was time for me to go back. A moment later I was lying in my bed once more with the boy and girl standing silently as before. The young girl said it was time for them to go, but they would be back.

I was left with a strong sense of cosiness and peace and simply accepted what happened to me without question. The boy and girl came back on quite a number of occasions afterwards, always playing with me in my bedroom and even tucking me in before they left. Then one day they stopped coming.

Were they real or was it all just my imagination working over-time? They looked and felt as solid as any of the children in the home. I never asked them their names. It simply never occurred to me to do so or seemed of any great importance. I called them my little angel friends. All I knew was they brought great happi-ness and joy into my life.

◈

I always seemed to be ill as a child, missing out on lots of picnics and parties and other events. It was frustrating lying in bed recov-ering while all the rest of the children at the home were having a good time. My sister Lottie always tried her best to make up for me missing out by bringing something back, such as a little piece of cake or sweeties, knowing this would cheer me up.

The annual Sunday school picnics were held during Easter in

the grounds of Fyvie Castle, about an hour's journey by bus from Aberdeen. They were always full of fun with all kinds of activities and races. I was useless at the three-legged race, tripping up more often than I ran and rolling about with my partner on the ground in fits of laughter. I wasn't much good at the egg and spoon race either. The egg fell off the spoon dozens of times before I eventually crossed the finishing line. Needless to say, I never won any races.

Although I looked forward to the picnic, I didn't enjoy the bus journey. I was a very bad traveller. The bus was always full to the brim, both with children from the church as well as the home, all eagerly anticipating the day to come. We set off from the church and headed north through the streets of Aberdeen and then out into the countryside. But as soon as the city was behind us, I felt my stomach begining to turn. I knew I was going to be sick. So I put my hand over my mouth. The kids sitting nearest to me noticed the colour draining away from my face.

"Stop the bus, driver. She's going to be sick!"

Other children took up the cry, leaving the bus driver little option but to pull over onto the side of the road. I only just made it in time as I jumped out and threw up in the grass verge. A few minutes later, we were back on the road once more heading towards our destination and all the kids were happy and excited again.

But a few miles further on, I felt queasy and the same cry went up and the bus came to a halt. Out I dashed to be sick a second time, much to the disgust of everyone aboard. My discomfort only grew as the outing progressed at a snail's pace, turning the hour-long journey into a marathon. By the time we arrived at Fyvie Castle, after I had thrown up at least another four or five times, most of the kids had lost their appetite for the picnic.

In the following years, whenever I boarded the bus, there were low murmerings of discontent and fed-up looks as I took my seat. By now, all the children knew what they were in for. One year, it was even decided I should travel up separately in a car. But even this master stroke failed miserably. I was still sick many times. Not surprisingly, the man who volunteered to take me never made the offer again.

I think everyone was mightily relieved the year I was too ill to go. But I experienced the strangest thing while lying in my bed recovering. I can't explain how exactly, but I found myself floating below the ceiling of a classroom looking down on many different tables with Easter cakes neatly laid out. Each of the cakes had a number placed at its side.

I felt as light as a feather and the view from above was exceptionally detailed and clear. I recognised Jean, who was brought up in the home for many years. She was at catering college now, studying to be a cook. Next to her was the house mother. They were both standing in the large room among a whole lot of people I didn't know. Although I heard the sound of many voices chattering away, I was only able to make out the words "prize" and "cake", nothing more. Somehow, I knew I was watching some competition taking place. Then I saw Jean go to a table, pick up a cake and take it to the top of the classroom and hold it up in front of everybody. There was a beaming smile on her face. The cake below me was covered in thick yellow icing and I noticed three little Easter chicks sitting on top surrounded by little green decorations of some kind. It looked so beautiful.

A few days later, when I was up and about and feeling much better, but not well enough to go to school, I overheard the house mother in the kitchen telling a member of staff about visiting the catering college and seeing Jean's cake. She described it as yellow with little chicks on top. Jean won the best cake prize.

But I already knew that, so I didn't give the conversation much thought. I never wondered how I could have been there when I was in my bed at the time. As an eight-year-old, I simply accepted the whole experience for what it was. However, I allowed myself a little smile, because I was there without the house mother knowing. And that gave me a real thrill.

Chapter Seven

THE HARSH SOUND of the playtime bell ringing disturbed the morning air. It was time to have some fun. Classrooms emptied within a minute and pupils jostled and pushed their way through bursting corridors before spilling out into the playground. The boys enjoyed the rough and tumble of football or played games of marbles by the school wall. The girls were altogether quieter. They played hopscotch or skipping or just hung about together in small groups of two or three. Frantic screams and squeals of delight filled the air, bringing the normally sedate city suburb to life.

The playground was cut off from the main road by a low wall. On the other side of the road, two or three small shops were plainly visible. There was not much in the way of cars passing or people walking by. About 500 yards down the road was the sprawling run-down housing estate where most of the schoolkids lived. My mother and most of my relatives also lived there. The contrast between the two areas was striking, the people living close to the school enjoying a far higher standard of living.

I was wandering around the playground by myself when I heard a lady's voice call out my name from across the street. Surprised, I looked over and saw two ladies standing on the pavement not far from the shops. They were both wearing light coloured headsquares and long dark coats down to their calves. One of the ladies beckoned me across the road. As I drew nearer, I recognised my mother.

The strong smell of alcohol made me feel sick. It came from her breath every time she opened her mouth to talk to me. Her words were slurred and I could barely understand her. I didn't know the lady who was with her. She was as drunk as my mother and wanted to buy me a box of chocolates.

"Oh aye, I'll awa' an' get them oot o' the wee shopie," she insisted, over and over. But she never went in to buy any. Instead, her mind seemed to drift and then focus on an entirely different topic.

"When you were a bairn, yer ma use tae hand you tae me," she said. "I used tae breastfeed you."

I didn't want to hear any more.

"Oh aye, yer ma would say, 'You tak' her,'" she mumbled on.

Her words rose and fell and then became barely audible as she tried hard to make herself understood. I felt disgusted by what this stranger was saying. But it was probably all true. Mother longed for the old ways. Whenever she felt the walls of Castlehill Barracks closing in on her, she took off on a bender and headed for Lightning Hill, one of the old traveller camping grounds. She used to disappear for days at a time, leaving my sister Gina, who was only 15, to look after my four brothers and sisters. My father was at sea at the time, working on the trawlers. All of this happened long before I was born.

By now I was feeling rather uncomfortable. All I wanted to do was to get as far away from my mother and her friend as I could. The school bell rang and gave me the excuse to leave. I blurted out a quick goodbye and ran smartly across the road without even a backward glance. It was a huge relief to leave these two drunks behind. I felt so happy to be back in school.

The unexpected meeting with my mother left a dark and dismal impression on me. It made me more determined to have nothing to do with her. She was not a mother to be proud of or someone to look up to. I felt hugely embarrassed and hated the thought of being related to her. It was the first and the last time my mother turned up at my school.

☙❧

Despite growing up with my brother Billy for many years, we never really knew each other. Little effort was made to build up any meaningful brother and sister relationship. It was the same with my sisters Mary Anne and Lottie. Yet, when it came to it, Billy was always protective towards me. He also enjoyed a fearsome reputation at school. Nobody messed with him.

Often I was asked, "Is Billy Whyte your brother?"

"Yes," I said, and that was enough to stop kids picking a fight with me.

But Billy didn't like having a sister. Girls skipped and played with dollies and didn't know anything about boys' games. So we never played much together. He showed no interest in me whatsoever and never let me join in anything he was doing. But I still needed him and wanted to share in the things he did. Begging and pleading just didn't work. He loved the pushing and shoving and the carrying on you only got playing with boys. Cry-baby girls were boring and much too soft. He paid the price for he was never out of plaster throughout our years together. There was hardly a bone in his body he didn't fracture or break. Sometimes he was also a bit on the cruel side and delighted in calling me "Tubby" or "Rolly Polly Dumpling" at every opportunity. One afternoon he was playing darts in the playroom with two of the other boys. I asked him if I could join in.

"No," he said. "No girls allowed."

"Why can't I have a game?" I asked.

"Because darts is a boys' game."

He wouldn't relent and I took the huff. I wanted to get my own back because he was so horrible. So I stood right in front of the dartboard to interrupt his aim.

"Move away from the dartboard!" he ordered.

But I wasn't budging and stood my ground.

"If you don't move away I'm going to throw this dart at you," replied Billy, in a deliberate tone of voice.

"I'm still not moving until you let me join in," I said, defiantly.

Billy ignored me and threw the dart towards the board. Suddenly, I felt a sharp stinging pain which made me howl and jump all over the place. The dart was sticking in my nose with blood pouring from my face. Billy looked at me unconcerned and continued throwing darts at the board. I ran out the playroom and around the back into the cloakroom screaming in agony. Luckily, a member of staff was already there, alerted by my screams and horrified to see the dart embedded in my nose. She quickly took charge of the situation and calmed me down. After gently pulling the dart out and cleaning the blood from my face, she covered the small wound left on my nose with some sticky plaster.

But my brother was as stubborn as I was. He refused to say sorry when I returned to the playroom a short while later. I stuck my plastered nose up in the air and didn't talk to him for the rest of the day. He wasn't even punished for what he did to me. This made me very angry. I started feeling resentful towards him. Every time he did something wrong, like smoking behind the garages, I got my own back by getting him sent to bed early as a punishment. Billy's lack of interest and attention towards me hurt me. The only time he seemed to notice me was when he was angry.

Around about this time, Billy started running away from the

home. I never knew anything about the strange man hanging outside the playground as he made his way to school in the morning. This went on for several days. Then one morning, the man shouted out his name and called him over and told him he was his father. Billy kept the meeting secret. No one knew about the plan they hatched so the authorities would send Billy back home to stay with my father and mother for good. The plan involved Billy running away from the home. The first time that happened, Billy disappeared for three days before being caught.

When I woke up one morning, there was no Billy to be seen anywhere. The house mother and staff were in a blind panic. I was worried, too. It was winter and freezing outside. I had visions of my brother wandering lost and alone, cold and hungry and surviving on raw turnips from the farmers' fields.

It was early evening and I was lying in my bed. Suddenly, I heard a commotion coming from downstairs. A man was bellowing out at the top of his voice. Curious, I crept out of bed to have a look and stood listening at the top of the stairs. Nobody noticed me. Peering over the highly polished bannister, I saw Billy with a man dressed in a white raincoat. Billy looked terrified. I was shocked to see the man screaming furiously at Billy and slapping him around. No one was doing anything about it either. The house mother was inside her sitting room and her door, only a few feet away, remained firmly shut the whole time. There was no way she could not have heard what was going on.

Billy was backed into a corner from which there was no escape and bravely took his punishment. I couldn't bear to watch. So I ran back into my room and jumped into bed, pulling the covers over my ears to drown out the man's shouting and Billy's screams. Thankfully, the whole incident didn't last very long. But for days afterwards, I felt very disturbed by what I witnessed. I never knew the name of the man although I found out later he was a children's officer from the local authority.

Despite all he suffered, Billy was determined to live with my mother and father. So he ran away again a few weeks later. Once more, I awoke to find my brother gone. This time, when he was caught and returned to the home, he was punched so hard he tumbled down a flight of stairs. Somehow my sister Lottie found out, even although she no longer lived at the home. She was furious and confronted the person responsible. But, of course, everything was denied. And as for me worrying over Billy being lost and alone and living on raw turnips from the fields, all along he was sitting warm and comfortable in my mother and father's house, smoking and drinking endless cups of tea. He was as safe as could be.

The plan must have worked for when he was 13, Billy and I were offered the chance to live with my mother and father at home. I was taken with Billy into the committee room and the house mother asked us what we wanted to do. Billy jumped at the chance. But I refused. I felt life would be much worse if I did. The feeling was overwhelming. As it turned out, my instinct, even at the age of 10, proved to be correct. My father and mother couldn't give up drinking. Often there was no money for food or anything else. Billy and my brother John, who was brought up in a different children's home, started breaking into bakery shops because they were starving. They were caught by the police and landed up in Borstal. But they escaped their miserable home life by joining the army as boy soldiers.

The first time I saw John was at Codona's, and then only for a few seconds. I loved going to the fair but I shouldn't have been there at all, without permission and on my own. But I managed to sneak away from the rest of the children from the home. They were playing on the beach and never knew I was gone.

I was watching a man trying to knock all the tin cans down at one of the many booths scattered about the fair. It didn't bother me very much. I had no money to spend. I was never given any anyway, so I was used to it. So I contented myself soaking in the exciting atmosphere which I loved. The hustle and bustle, the chaos and colours and smells and music were such a contrast to the rigid predictable existence which was my daily experience at the home.

The man was disappointed not being able to knock the tins down at the first go and dug ever deeper into his pockets. He was determined to go home with some kind of prize, no matter how cheap and tacky. I moved on to a shooting gallery and stood hypnotized by the small yellow ducks moving endlessly across the back of the booth in perfect time. But no one seemed to be able to hit the required number of ducks to win the prize, a giant teddy. Two pellets hit the mark easily, but the third one always seemed to go astray. No one seemed to notice, or care.

Suddenly, the spell was broken by a tap on my shoulder. On looking around, a young teenage boy thrust a small rag doll into my hand. I was taken aback by the stranger's action.

"I'm your brother John," he said.

He walked off and was quickly lost from view, swallowed up in the milling crowds. It was all unexpected. I didn't know what to make of it as I looked at the rag doll he must have won as a prize. How did he know me? How come I had a brother I never knew existed up until this moment? No one had ever mentioned him before. The questions kept coming as I made my way home still clutching the doll, which I placed carefully down on the pillow on my bed. I thought we didn't even look alike. My hair was brown and his was ginger in colour. My nose was turned up and his was straight. But it was still a nice feeling, knowing I had two brothers instead of just the one.

I kept the meeting secret because I was afraid of getting into trouble. It was bad enough going to the fair in the first place. But, if the house mother knew I also met my brother, even although it was John who found me, I would surely have been punished more severely. So I kept quiet about the whole affair, not even mentioning anything to Billy.

It would be another four years or so before I saw John again. He turned up out of the blue one afternoon along with Billy while I was in the playroom. They both wore black blazers and looked really smart. I noticed how tall they were. It was the first time I'd seen Billy since he left the home some three years previously, when he was 13. Now he was all grown up and a fine young man. I was over the moon seeing them and very happy Billy had also found John, who was his older brother. John grew up in Craigielea Children's Home and knew nothing about any of us. I was delighted to be able to meet him properly at last. When we first met at the fair, John only spoke four words to me. Now we had the chance to get to know each other and to make up for all the lost time.

As I held on tightly to both their arms, chatting away to my two brothers on either side of me, it was a really nice feeling. For the very first time, I felt I had a real family. But that special precious moment of joy was to be short lived. A member of staff burst into the playroom demanding they both leave immediately because they hadn't made an appointment to see me. John tried to explain they were both in the army and on leave and had to go back to rejoin their units in the morning. But the member of staff was having none of it. My heart sank as they reluctantly turned and left the playroom. I felt a deep sense of loss as I watched them walking down the driveway and disappearing out of the gates. How I had longed for such a moment which now was so cruelly snatched away from me. It would have been nice spending just one hour of one afternoon with them both. But it wasn't meant to be. Depression settled over me for days afterwards.

John and Billy were sent off on active service to Northern Ireland. When I left the home a few years later I didn't know where they were stationed and had no way of finding out. I wasn't to see them again until many years later. By then, both had settled down far away from Scotland with families of their own.

No one thought it was important to tell me how to get in touch with them, or with any of my other brothers and sisters. There were three younger brothers I never knew I had. I also knew nothing about James, the oldest of all my brothers, or Gina, who was to die before I ever got the chance to meet her. Eventually I found Lottie again, but only after knocking on many doors.

But the sadness which formed such a large part of my life while growing up in the home was nothing out of the ordinary. The consequences of tragedy were all around me, every single day. You smelt it. The bedroom I shared with three other girls always stank of pee every morning. It was the same with the little boys' room and the big girls' room. You couldn't escape the smell at the breakfast table either. Children who slept without any pyjama bottoms in soaking wet beds simply put on their clothes in the morning without washing. Then they came down to breakfast as usual. It was all part of the routine, just like the house mother's impatient thoughtless order.

"Put your hands up all those who wet the bed!"

Meekly, hands rose slowly as if trying to escape her steely gaze. But it was no use. There was no hiding from the piercing eyes or the embarrassment they now deeply felt. Next came the expected pronouncement.

"All those who put their hands up are going to bed early tonight," she said, without neither hint of compassion nor understanding.

There was only acceptance of the punishment meted out with such dismal regularity. The children I lived with all had deep emotional problems and impossible mental scars. But there was no one they could turn to for help. They came from all over the country to find themselves among total strangers. If the routine was rigid and disciplined, they soon found the environment of the home devoid of any meaningful love or support. Sometimes they stayed with us for only a few weeks or months and then they were gone. Others stayed for years.

Margaret was quite typical, having found her mother lifeless one morning with her head stuck in the gas oven. Sarah discovered her mother hanging from the stair banisters when she came home from school one afternoon. Others lost one or both parents in car smashes or watched helplessly as their mother died slowly of cancer.

I had also been like them until only a few months before, always wetting the bed every single night. But, unlike the other children, my bed-wetting was deliberate. It was either that or face the ghost of the previous house mother. Billy told me he saw her coming towards him when he raided the pantry one night. I was terrified for months afterwards. The toilet was a long way off at the other end of the home. To get to it, you went down a small flight of stairs past the big girls' room, then down a long, winding staircase leading to the cloakroom. The toilet was next to it. I wasn't brave enough to venture down there on my own in the dark. So I preferred the punishment I knew would be coming in the morning.

Life only got worse for the bed-wetters, as the house mother delighted in calling them. I was settling down to sleep one evening. Just as as the last rays of the setting sun were creeping out through the small attic window in my room, she suddenly barged in unannounced carrying something in her hands. She made a beeline over to where Margaret slept, which was in the bed opposite mine at the bottom of the room.

"Now, all bed-wetters will wear this," she said, sternly. As she leaned over Margaret lying in bed, the house mother swiftly pulled back the covers, folded a large white square cloth into a triangle and then ordered her to lift her bottom up from the mattress. Then she quickly slipped the cloth underneath and secured it by means of two safety pins. Margaret was now wearing a nappy. I couldn't believe it, a young girl forced to wear a nappy. I was shocked.

"It's only babies that wet the bed. Until you stop wetting the bed, you'll wear a nappy at night," said the house mother, in a mocking voice. Then she left and went from room to room and put a nappy on all the other children who wet the bed. Margaret pulled the bed covers tightly into her body, buried her face deep in the pillow and never uttered a word. I felt extremely lucky to have escaped the humiliation because I was no longer scared to go to the toilet at night on my own.

If the house mother thought punishing the bed-wetters by treating them like babies would work, she was wrong. It didn't. Those children still woke up every morning soaking wet. After a few weeks of the nappies, they went back to wearing nothing except their pyjama tops. They were wakened up in the middle of the night and led down the stairs to the toilet, naked from the waist down. When they came back, they climbed into soaking beds knowing another punishment awaited them in the morning.

Chapter Eight

THE USUAL ROUTE HOME from primary school took me through a small area of grass-covered waste ground used for the dumping of old cars, tyres and other junk. It was a dirty forgotten place where every kind of litter was discarded on a daily basis, including dozens of sweetie wrappers dropped by kids using the waste ground as a short cut.

One afternoon, as I was walking home through the waste ground with my brother Billy, we saw a young-looking man with black curly hair who was standing next to one of the abandoned cars. The man was crouched down with a bicycle pump in his hand and was furiously pumping air into the ground instead of the car tyre a few inches away. Beads of sweat dripped off his face as he cursed and grew redder with each passing second. I asked him what he was doing but he just ignored me. I couldn't understand why he was pumping air into the ground instead of the tyre. Billy and I started to giggle. The giggles gave way to fits of laughter and the man still carried on as if we were invisible.

After a few minutes, Billy started to get bored and tried to pull me away, but I wasn't having any of it. I didn't like being told what to do. Besides, this was so funny and I couldn't stop laughing. So he gave up and left me to make his own way home. A few minutes later, even I had had enough. So I turned away leaving the man still pumping the ground furiously. I saw Billy in the distance, still dawdling up the road.

Suddenly, without warning, I was pinned to the ground, barely able to take in what was happening. A dark mass lay on top of me and strong filthy hands were around my neck, choking the life out of me. I couldn't move or struggle as my body felt crushed under a huge weight. In my mind, I was screaming but no sound left me as I struggled for breath. Seconds turned into an eternity as time slowed down to a crawl. I was moments away from blackness. Then, from some point far away in the distance, I became aware of a thumping noise, and then a woman's voice screaming frantically "Get off her!" over and over.

The vice-like grip around my neck loosened slightly and the weight pinning my body shifted. From the swirling confused mist of semi-consciousness, I saw a thick heavy broom handle moving in a lazy arc through the air in slow motion. As it drifted in and out of view, I heard a dull thump, thump, thump and the weight on top of me lessened each time. I caught glimpses of Billy, who seemed to be punching and kicking out at something.

My focus sharpened and suddenly there was no more weight on top of me. I recognised the lady helping me up. She had just recently moved into the green-painted house nearby, which overlooked the waste ground. Sometimes I talked to her two daughters, Rhoda and Rhonda, who were a year or two older than me. They were missing their father a lot who was away working in Africa.

I was in deep shock. My legs were wobbly and my throat hurt so much I couldn't talk. The lady helped me the 100 yards or so to the home, encouraging me all the way with gentle words of kindness and support. A few seconds after the front door bell was rung, the house mother appeared. The lady explained what had happened and the house mother told me to go through and play with the other children. She barely acknowledged or registered any concern over the incident or showed me any sympathy whatsoever, simply calling the police.

The police appeared a short time later. In a shaky voice, which was still hoarse and barely above a whisper, I told them as best I could exactly what happened, which they noted down in their notebooks. All the while, the house mother just stood there, silent, never saying a word.

Next day, the incident was the talk of the school playground because the man lived in the same area as some of the kids. They saw him being lifted by the police. In the weeks following, the house mother never mentioned anything at all about the attack or asked me how I was coping. Life at the home just carried on as normal as if nothing had ever happened. A few weeks later, I heard from kids in the playground the man appeared in court and was jailed.

I often thought what would have happened if I had been walking home alone that day, or if the lady had not been looking out the window at just the right time. I was thankful for the bravery she showed, using the broom handle to save my life. I was also grateful to Billy, who without a moment's thought for his own safety, launched himself at the man. Without them both, I probably would have been killed.

⚬⟡⚬

In 1964, Aberdeen was virtually brought to a standstill when it was hit by a typhoid outbreak, which at the time was the largest in modern British history. The city felt under seige for weeks as more than 500 people became infected with the dangerous bacteria, later traced to a can of contaminated corned beef from Argentina which was sold in a local supermarket.

It was only days after my ninth birthday when the first victims became ill with the disease and movement everywhere was restricted. Like other institutions and buildings across the city the home, with its eighteen kids, was put under quarantine. It meant no school, no church, no visitors, as we were locked up behind the steel gates for weeks.

But it turned out to be so much worse for us than that. On rainy days, we were confined to the playroom, which was no more than an extension tagged on to the back of the main building. It was a dismal place with yellow painted walls and a bare lino-covered floor. There was no form of heating in the playroom, or curtains on windows, or chairs to sit on, or pictures to brighten up the walls. Broken toys and board games with pieces missing lay scattered across the floor providing the only stimulation. So we quickly became restless and bored and fights and quarrels broke out with monotonous regularity over the smallest sleight or triviality. On one occasion, I got into an argument with my cousin Eddie and ended up bursting his nose. One of the children ran out of the playroom to report us and a member of staff stormed in.

"Right, you two, bed!" she roared, not interested in who was responsible for starting the fight or why.

Some children handled the tension more easily than others. I had been brought up in care from a small child and was now so conditioned by rules, regulations and restrictions that I expected little out of life. There were never any visits from any surviving parent or relative to look forward to for me. But others looked forward to such visits. It was all that kept them going. Now they found themselves in the same situation as me for the very first time. Once they enjoyed a good family life on the outside until some tragedy took everything away. Now the typhoid epidemic robbed them of even the little family contact they had left. So it was much harder for them.

The quarantine restrictions dragged on day after day and then week after week. The monotony was broken only when meals were served. We were shouted through from the playroom, or from the playground if the weather allowed us to go outside. Each day ended with a couple of hours watching television followed by bed.

But Sunday was different. Our souls still needed saving and since we couldn't go to the church, the church came to us. The house mother organised and led a church service in the dining room, complete with prayers and hymn singing. She even recorded the service on a tape recorder. I never knew why she did this. The service lasted an hour and a half and was followed by dinner. Then we were all thrown back into the playroom once more.

The typhoid outbreak began some time during the second week of May and by the beginning of June more than fifty people a day were being admitted to hospital suspected of having contracted the disease. Routine operations were cancelled at many hospitals where wards were cleared out and turned over to treating cases. Some hospitals were even turned into temporary typhoid hospitals and nothing else.

Thanks to the efforts of the many health workers across the city and from further afield, the outbreak reached its peak within a month. On 17 June, the all-clear was given and normal life slowly returned. At the end of the month the Queen paid a visit to thank all those who helped in bringing the epidemic under control. It was also a signal that Aberdeen was now safe for visitors. Over 40,000 people lined the streets to welcome Her Majesty. Eventually, restrictions were lifted at the home, too, and we were all glad to be able to walk out the gates once more and to go to school and see our classmates. The six weeks seemed like a lifetime.

But although normality and routine returned quickly, nothing was quite the same ever again. It was as if we were forgotten by the world. My sixpence pocket money, which I got now and again, dried up completely, so there were no more visits to the nearby sweetshop which I looked forward to on a Saturday morning. I never went to the swimming pool or cinema again and theatre visits and other outings became fewer and farther between. The little things which made life a little more bearable slowly disappeared, adding to the resentment I felt growing inside me.

⁊

Some months later, all the newspapers in Aberdeen were full of speculation. For weeks they asked the same question: "Who is Little Miss X?" Little Miss X or Little Miss Anonymous were the names they gave to the young child chosen in secrecy who was to switch on the Christmas lights in the city. This had never happened before and because it was a "first", it was big news. Even if they somehow got to know her name, they couldn't legally disclose it anyway. But that didn't stop the stories or members of the public trying to guess who she was. All anyone knew for certain was that Little Miss X lived in one of the local orphanages.

Little Miss X turned out to be me. But I never knew who she was right up until the night before the event. I prayed for a miracle for weeks, for something special to happen in my life. Little did I know how spectacularly my prayers were to be answered. I was to have fifteen minutes of fame, yet no one would ever know my name.

The first hint or clue something special was about to happen to me sailed over the top of my head. It was just too impossible sounding, so I didn't take it seriously. I was sitting in the school dinner hall next to a boy called Jack. He never looked very clean at the best of times with his blond cropped hair and snotty nose. His clothes always seemed like they were in need of a wash. I didn't like him very much after he freaked us all out one lunchtime

when he was sitting next to some kid who upset him and he
erupted. We heard an almighty thud from further down the hall
making us all turn around to see what was happening. He was like
a madman, throwing chairs and upsetting tables and shouting at
the top of his voice. Teachers and dinner ladies rushed over to take
control of the situation which must have lasted for a good half
hour. Eventually, they managed to calm him down. Now he was
sitting beside me, a few days later, as good as gold but I was still
rather wary of him.

We were eating soup when Jack paused a moment between noisy
slurps and blurted out, "You're putting on the Christmas lights!"

I think I stared at him with a silly blank expression on my face,
wondering what he was talking about. "What do you mean?"

"My dad's a councillor and he told me you're putting the lights
on," he said, with absolute certainty in his voice.

"Right," I said, not believing a word of it, for there was no mention
of Christmas lights happening anywhere that I knew about.

"You are, you are," he repeated in response to the disbelieving
look and lack of enthusiasm in my face.

The Christmas holidays were only a matter of a few weeks away.
The house mother told me one morning to tell the teacher I had
to go to the dentist and needed to be let out early from school. So I
did what I was asked. Later that afternoon, I found myself looking
around the shops in the city centre with the house mother, never
going anywhere near a dentist. The next morning, I was told to tell
the teacher I had another dental appointment, but this time she
was a little bit suspicious, not quite believing me.

"Are you telling me lies?" she asked.

"No. You can phone the house mother if you don't believe me."

Since she couldn't prove otherwise, the teacher let me leave
school early again. Once more, I was looking around the shops
with the house mother, but this time trying on shoes and clothes.

I kept wondering why she had me telling lies to the teacher.

The following Saturday, the house mother said I was to go out with her eldest daughter but she wouldn't say to where. Naturally, I didn't question the order but just did as I was told. Her daughter took me to a hairdresser's shop in a rather posh part of the city which catered for only the best clientele. She told me to take a seat on one of the plush red leather chairs because she needed to talk to the stylist on her own. Minutes passed and there was no sign of the house mother's daughter and I grew quickly bored and started to fidget. When at last she appeared we caught the bus back to the home.

I still didn't realise anything unusual was going on even when later on that evening I was unexpectedly summoned into the house mother's private sitting room, something that just never ever happened. I thought at first I must be in trouble, but the house mother was rather nice to me and told me to sit down on the carpet.

"Look at me carefully," the house mother said, waving her lower arm slowly and gracefully back and forward through the air. "I want you to learn to wave like the Queen."

So I sat there for half an hour waving my arm slowly back and forward, following the house mother's movements precisely, until she was satisfied in her mind I had got the wave perfect. We did this every night for four nights in a row. On the last night, the house mother said she had something to tell me. I suddenly felt nervous.

"Tomorrow night, you are going to be switching on the Christmas lights," she said.

I looked at her with a blank expression, having no idea what she meant. She was excited about something, but I wasn't. After all, I hadn't a clue about all the speculation or build-up going on for weeks because I never got to read any newspapers. Nobody told me anything, or at least anything I believed.

Next day, I was back at the posh hairdresser's shop I had been at only a few days before. But this time my hair was being cut and styled. I was the centre of attention and lapped it all up like a sponge. The hairdresser even sprinkled silver dust through my hair, which I loved.

Back at the home, I went upstairs to find a pretty party frock and matching shoes waiting for me, all laid out neatly in my bedroom. A few minutes later, I was finished dressing and the house mother took me through to the kitchen where my brother Billy was standing.

"Doesn't Patsy look pretty?" the house mother asked Billy.

He looked at me with a grudging smile. It was plain to see he was jealous. He was also rather annoyed to be going to the Christmas lights ceremony in a double-decker bus instead of going there with me. The bus would be one of several buses filled with children from other children's homes in the city. It would form part of a large procession of decorated floats and pipe bands and displays of all kinds.

Before I knew it, the bus arrived and all the children piled on and then they were gone, leaving the home feeling rather lonely and empty. The house mother told me to wait in the kitchen and a minute or two later she appeared there carrying a beautiful deep-red velvet cloak with a white fur-trimmed hood which she told me to put around myself. Then she took a white fluffy muffler from out of a box and placed it around my neck and I felt very pretty. I looked a bit like Little Red Riding Hood.

Shortly afterwards, the front door bell rang. I was led by a uniformed chauffeur to a gleaming Rolls Royce parked in the driveway. As he opened the door to let me in I saw the Lord and Lady Provost of Aberdeen were already sitting in the back seat. The Provost, who gave me a warm friendly smile which immediately put me at ease, looked very important and dignified with his gold chains of office around his neck. His wife was dressed up all posh in a fancy hat which matched the colour of her expensive coat. She was rather stuck-up.

The Rolls Royce left the home and glided through the streets of Aberdeen heading towards the city centre. As we slowly drove through King Street and then George Street, crowds were gathering on either side of the road.

"Wave to the people!" the Lady Provost said suddenly, in a rather sharpish tone.

Then it dawned on me, like some piece of a puzzle falling into place. Suddenly I understood why I had spent so many hours learning to wave like the Queen. I was a mere spectator up until that moment, watching events unfold around me, yet not taking part in any of it. I was just sitting in the back seat of the Rolls Royce, with its plush ivory white leather seats and mahogany panels, enjoying looking out the window. But the crowds lining the road on a bitterly cold night were there just to see me. It was incredible. As we drove slowly along Aberdeen's famous Union Street, the main thoroughfare running through the heart of the city, which had been emptied of all traffic except for our Rolls Royce, the crowds on each side swelled from a few hundred people to thousands upon thousands, all waving and cheering madly. With every passing yard the noise only got louder, merging into one continuous deafening roar by the time we came to a halt in front of the Music Hall, our final destination.

I stepped out of the Rolls Royce and walked up the steps into the Music Hall flanked by the Lord and Lady Provost. They led me through to a large room where there were lots of sandwiches, finger foods and cakes of all descriptions, all laid out on long tables covered with white starched tablecloths. Milling around were smartly dressed people I didn't know, huddled together in small groups and engaged in deep conversations. I felt a little uncomfortable as my eyes wandered around the room. It was a beautiful room with a high ornamental ceiling and large windows draped in rich red velvet curtains which broke the white of the walls. I was relieved to see the house mother's eldest daughter enter the room and make her way towards me.

"I'm your lady in waiting," she said.

I had no idea what she meant but I was very glad to see a familiar face. She looked very pretty. There were small blue flowers in her jet-black hair which was swept high off her face. She normally dressed in a blouse and mini skirt and I'd never seen her before in a smart two piece Tweed suit. She didn't look out of place as she chatted happily away with the toffs and dignitaries of Aberdeen.

It was getting nearer the moment for me to switch on the lights and a lady's voice broke through the chatter in the room.

"Come with me," she said. "It's time to go. Just follow me."

The room fell silent. Dozens of pairs of eyes followed my every movement as I was led through a door and out onto the balcony. Suddenly, I was blinded by dozens of flash bulbs going off from every direction and deafened by the wall of sound coming up to greet me from the crowds standing in the darkness behind barriers on the opposite side of the street.

I was followed onto the balcony by the Lord Provost and by other important dignitaries, including the Lord Mayor of London. A small raised platform was specially built for me otherwise the balcony wall would have hidden me from the crowds. A rostrum was positioned at the front of the platform and on top was a simple toggle switch with a microphone nearby. Without a trace of nervousness, I stepped up on the platform with the Lord Provost at my side.

"Say a few words," said the Lord Provost, unexpectedly.

No one told me I was to speak to the crowds. Now, for the first time, I felt some butterflies in my stomach as I moved my face towards the microphone. The Lord Provost looked at me intently, his eyes telling me to get a move on, but under the pressure I found it hard to think of anything to say.

"I wish you all a merry Christmas and a happy New Year."

I said the words without realising it but they were perfect for the occasion. The Lord Provost beckoned me to flick the switch down, which I did, lighting up the whole of Union Street in a blaze of glorious colour. As flash bulbs popped once more and the crowd roared out their approval, I heard the sound of pipes in the distance. The procession was starting. The sound of the pipes grew louder and louder amid the growing buzz and excitement. Small flakes of snow were falling gently as I gazed up at the lights shining high above me. I was hypnotised by the beauty of it all. The large fluffy flakes drifted slowly downwards in the cold night air, glistening and sparkling in a rainbow of colours, each one reflecting for a moment the lights behind before melting into the pavement. I wanted to remember this magical fairy-tale scene for ever.

The pipe major, dressed in full Highland regalia and swinging his mace proudly at the head of a long column of pipers and drummers, was now almost level with the balcony. With kilts swishing and dozens of pairs of brogues marking perfect time to the beat of the music, the pipe band marched swiftly past and disappeared out of view.

Behind them followed a procession of brightly decorated floats, each one carrying anything up to a dozen people. They were all waving happily to the crowds. Every float represented a different organisation or charity or business which was well known in the city. I returned the enthusiastic waves as each slowly passed in front of the balcony.

The tail end of the procession was made up of five or six double-decker buses filled with kids from Aberdeen's children's homes. I tried hard to spot which one held the children from my home but

I couldn't make out any familiar faces through the windows. Before I had any real time to register anything, each bus had passed by me and was out of sight, leaving me feeling a bit disappointed.

When the last bus passed the balcony the procession was over. The spectators started to make their way homewards. Many of them had been standing behind the barriers for more than an hour and were now glad to be leaving. But quite a number darted across the empty street to get a better look at me. As they got nearer, I recognised several kids from my school.

"What was it like, what was it like?" they shouted up at me.

I never got the chance to reply because I was whisked back into the Music Hall to the large room where the dignitaries were already sitting down enjoying the start of a slap-up meal. But I felt too uncomfortable to join them. They were far too toffee-nosed for my liking. Instead, I went over to the tables where the food I saw earlier was laid out and although starving, I stopped myself from diving in because I was acutely aware of the house mother's daughter. She was watching my every move. So I made sure my manners were beyond reproach as I daintily filled a plate with a selection of sandwiches and cakes.

Before I knew it, the evening was over for me. It was time to take my leave of the Music Hall. Following the Lord and Lady Provost down the steps, I saw the chauffeur was already waiting beside the open doors of the Rolls Royce and I climbed aboard. The Rolls Royce once more glided down Union Street which was now quiet and deserted with litter strewn across the pavements on either side.

The Lord Provost pulled out a small red box and handed it to me. I opened it to see a gold necklace with a small crystal lantern in the middle. It was given to me by the City of Aberdeen to mark the occasion. I took it out of the box and held it up and watched the light through the crystal lantern changing into many different colours.

"Stop!" said the Lord Provost, suddenly.

The Rolls Royce driver was a bit surprised, as we all were. The Lord Provost quickly rolled down the window and shouted over to a man on the other side of the street. The old man, a cripple, had been a spectator watching in the crowd and was now struggling through the snow on his own, the last straggler to make his way homewards.

"Get in," said the Lord Provost, opening the door for him.

With a bit of an effort and a helping hand from the Lord Provost, the elderly man got in and sat down in the seat opposite. He was glad to be out of the cold. It seemed to me the Lord Provost knew the man who appeared to have fallen on hard times. Judging by the conversation they were having, they were old friends. The Lord Provost's wife seemed a little bit put out by this unexpected end to the evening, pretending not to listen or care. I was too busy admiring my new necklace.

The Rolls Royce pulled quietly into the driveway of the home and I thanked the Lord Provost for everything before going inside. The house mother was waiting for me but never asked whether I enjoyed the evening or how it all went. After shutting the front door, she told me to hand over the necklace and then go straight up to bed.

More than six years were to pass before I saw the necklace again. I telephoned the home after I left and asked for it back. The house mother posted it on to me without even a letter or short note or anything. Some time later, the necklace sadly disappeared.

My beautiful cloak and muffler were taken off me and placed in a large cardboard box. The box was kept in the house mother's bedrooom. It lay on top of a wardrobe gathering dust for years. I never saw the cloak or muffler again. Nor did I ever wear the party frock or the shoes which were later given to another girl in the home while I struggled to walk about in badly fitting second-hand shoes.

I was the centre of attention the following day at school. All my classmates had seen me up on the balcony and were now dying to know what it was like. I know my teacher was very proud of me. She even pinned a newspaper cutting up on the classroom wall for all to see. Later on that night, I was allowed to stay up late to watch the event on the ITN television news programme *News At Ten*. I couldn't believe I was really looking at myself. It all felt very weird.

My appearance on television ignited the whole hullabaloo all over again at school the next day. Eventually, after telling and then re-telling the story yet again, the attention started getting a bit tiresome. Eventually, I was completely fed up with it all and refused to answer any more questions. I was glad when the weeks turned to months and my fifteen minutes of fame gradually faded quietly into the background, destined to be forgotten.

⚜

More than twenty-five years later, I was to be reminded of the whole evening again in a quite unexpected way. I was living in London at the time. My eldest daughter was doing a school essay about parents. Although I only ever mentioned my switching on the lights once or twice in passing, nevertheless she decided to write about it. So she asked me for more details. The next day she returned home from school rather excited.

"You'll never guess what," she said. "My teacher remembers you switching on the lights! He always wondered who the little girl was. Now he knows and he's delighted."

I don't think I believed it myself. Someone still remembered me after all those years. Thinking about it, I suppose I was served up as the perfect Christmas image, unforgettable, pure and white as the snow falling on Union Street that evening. But no one ever looked much beyond that.

Of all the little girls who might have been chosen to switch on the lights, fate chose me. Was that just a coincidence and nothing more, or was there some unseen hand at work, guiding my life? Because I have experienced such a lot over the years, I tend to favour the latter more and more. Maybe I was meant to see the Lord Provost's act of kindness in helping the crippled man. A man in his lofty position could have just driven by. No one would have known. But he didn't and it's something I've always remembered. Maybe that was the real lesson I learned that night.

Chapter Nine

THE LOCAL PARK was no more than a stone's throw away from the home. It was a favourite haunt of the local kids, especially during the long-drawn-out days of summer. Hard-up parents were thankful for the park because it didn't cost them anything. It was somewhere to send their kids to play. They were safe there and at the same time, out from under their feet.

I noticed the park attendant hadn't been around for a week or two, so the older kids were getting away with picking on the younger children or sometimes even battering them. The park attendant, or parkie as he was known to us, always wore a grey tunic with silver buttons down the front and a matching grey cap. He was a middle-aged man who reminded me more of a bus conductor. Although strict if he had to be, he was also very fair. He always took the time to get to know the children who played regularly in the park, happily chatting away to them for hours on end. Out came a sticky plaster or two to cover any cuts and grazes if needed. But watch out if you dared vandalise the swings or damage the flower beds or fight or swear or break any of the park's many bylaws. Then he showed his other face, which was always quick to banish any miscreant from the park.

I was holding on to the the maypole, spinning round and round trying to fly through the air. Curiosity got the better of me when I heard the sounds of laughter and muffled voices coming from some thickly growing bushes nearby. So I sneaked over to find out what was going on. The area of bushes was separated from the play area by a low wire fence. It ran the whole length of the park. I thought I recognised the voices. Carefully, I parted the bushes to get a better look and saw two naked bodies lying one on top of the other. On the ground beside them were two neat piles of clothing.

"Keep going, keep going!" said the girl, who I immediately recognised as Gabby, one of the teenagers from the home.

The boy lying on top of her was James. His face looked red and sweaty. He was also from the home. Even although I didn't exactly understand what they were up to, instinctively I felt what I was watching was wrong. Seeing their naked bodies made me feel very uncomfortable. Nakedness was considered dirty and unchristian and therefore not acceptable at the home. But here they both were, hiding, being secretive, doing things they were not supposed to do away from prying eyes. They never knew I was watching them. My discovery left me in a bit of a quandary. Should I report them? Should I tell the house mother? If I did, what would I say? I knew the trouble they both would be in if I did so. So I decided to say nothing.

Later in the evening, they were both sitting apart at the dinner table, carrying on as normal with not a hint of the secret love affair. They hid it all so well, from the rest of the children, the staff and the house mother. I assumed the affair continued throughout the rest of the summer because they constantly visited the park. Occasionally I heard the sound of laughter coming from the bushes. But I never went over to investigate.

When the long summer finally came to a close, the secret love affair also ended. Gabby and James left the home the following year to make their own separate ways in the world. I never saw either of them again. My primary school days were also over, too. In a few days, I was due to begin high school, which I wasn't looking forward to very much.

As for the parkie, he was phased out along with all the other park attendants across the city. No longer would we ever feel quite so safe, innocently playing childish games all day in the park until the last of the evening light forced us away. It was the end of an era.

ᚑᚈᚑ

High school proved every bit as bad as I feared. Every year felt more miserable and humiliating than the last one and the only day I looked forward to was the one when I could officially leave. But that was still several years away. As I grew from a child to a teenager, my identity was stripped away more and more. Even when visitors came to the home, Billy and I were always referred to as the Whytes.

My hair was cut short, but not by a proper hairdresser. I wore a grey school cardigan and grey socks. The other girls at my school were dressed in modern cords and fashionable tops. They talked about the discos they'd been to or the youth clubs run by the different schools or about meeting each other at night times. Boyfriends were a constant topic of conversation. So were the best ploys to use to dump them in order to go out with someone else they fancied.

Long hair was becoming the fashion and most of the girls had a grown-up teenage look. But not me. It was then I realised I was different. I had none of the experiences they had. Each day was the same as every other day, nothing to get excited about. It was straight home from school and if I was more than ten or fifteen minutes late, I was put to bed after tea. Nobody from school was allowed to call on me and I wasn't allowed to go out to a disco or youth club. I had never been shopping for new clothes or shoes except the once, when I put on the Christmas lights. It was hard to engage in any conversation. I knew my classmates felt as uncomfortable around me as I did around them.

One afternoon, as I left the high school, a group of kids from the school followed me out of the gates. They chanted "Homey kid" all the way back to the home. Every day, they kept up the same taunts, both in the playground and on the way home from school. I was upset and scared but there was nothing I could do. There was no one I could turn to. It just underlined how different I was from everyone else. Even the teachers forgot my name was Patsy. Instead, they referred to me, and the other children who lived with me, as the kids from the home. We were not like the other pupils at the school. We were a separate group with no individual identities, little better than a pack of animals.

Mrs Dawson was an exception, a kind and sweet lady who gave me the responsibility of taking care of the plants in the classroom. One year, she let me take them home during the summer holidays so I could look after them. I felt really happy and useful because I knew how much her plants meant to her. It was the last day of term and as I proudly carried the plants away, someone in the playground told me they knew my mother. They lived in the same street as her. I handed over one of the pot plants and asked them to give it to her. Why I did that, I don't know. I took really good care of the plants and at the end of the summer holidays brought them all back to Mrs Dawson's class. But she never came back. Months afterwards, I heard she died of cancer.

Mr Hunter was my English teacher. He stared at everyone over the top of his small half glasses. I didn't like his class. On Tuesday mornings, he asked the class for money for school assembly. Every pupil reached into their purses or pockets and money jingled as they pulled out twopence to put in a small basket passed down each row of desks. I dreaded the moment the basket was handed to me. Each week, Mr Hunter demanded to know where my money was and squinted at me accusingly. Each week, I said the same thing back. I didn't have any.

"You make sure you have it for next Tuesday!" he replied, in a sharp, grumpy tone.

And every time, Louise and some of the other pupils sensed my humiliation and embarrassment. "I'll pay for her!" they said, before putting money in the basket on my behalf.

Mr Hunter never once thought to ask me why I never had any money. I begged the house mother every Monday night for money for assembly. But her reply was always the same. "You tell them charity begins at home!"

It was different for Eddie. He was also in the home and in the same class as me. But he had a father who took him out every Sunday. Eddie's dad always made sure he had money for the tuck shop and for assembly. I had no one to give me any. If I had, I would gladly have handed it over to stop the humiliation in front of the whole class.

But it wasn't just assembly you needed money for. You also had to pay for the ingredients used in cookery class. I liked cooking, even although I was a terrible cook. My teacher was Mrs Brown, a middle-aged lady with short grey hair which had a slight wave through it. She was strict but always fair and doubled up as the sewing teacher. I told Mrs Brown I forgot whenever she asked me where my ingredients and money for the lesson were. It was a feeble excuse to use at the best of times. I used the same excuse practically every week because I couldn't think of anything else to say. She started to lose patience with me, thinking I wasn't interested in the lessons at all. But nothing was further from the truth. At the end of the lesson, she gave us the list of ingredients and the cost for next week. She never saw my embarrassment, although it was plainly visible, or understood I was making up excuses for the home.

It was just like Monday nights, with the same ritual played out once more and with the same predictable outcome. I asked the house mother for the ingredients and money and she dismissed my request, pointing out once more how charity began at home. She used the same phrase week after week, then month after month, knowing full well how difficult it made life for me at school. It was her favourite phrase, the answer to everything, the excuse not to spend a single penny on the likes of someone like me. I was convinced of that.

One day, I got fed up with it all. I was desperate. Before going to school, I slipped into the kitchen without being seen and made my way down the steps leading to the food larder. It was a large room with shelves stacked full of tinned foods of all kinds. I was four the last time I set foot in there. It was my first day at the home.

As well as tins of fruit and meat, there were bags of sugar, rows of packet tea, flour and everything imaginable. It was like going to the corner shop with all the goodies on display, all within reach, mine for the taking. I scanned the shelves looking for the tin of mandarins I needed for the cookery lesson. Quickly jumping from one neatly stacked row of tins to another, my attention was drawn to a brightly coloured label. The word "Mandarins" in large letters screamed out at me. Without thinking about the trouble I could be in, I nervously snatched at the tin of forbidden fruit and stuffed it under my school jumper out of sight. Looking around to make sure no one was watching me, I hurredly slipped on my school coat and the deception was complete. I felt both a strong sense of relief and elation as I crept quietly out of the kitchen to join the other kids in the cloakroom. No one missed me.

The house mother was ushering the kids out the door in single file so they wouldn't be late for school. It was the usual routine and I waited my turn in the queue. Just as I reached the door, a sharp voice behind me shouted out, stopping me dead in my tracks.

"What are you hiding under your coat?" the house mother demanded angrily.

Oh God, I thought. This is it. She knows.

"Open up your coat!" she ordered.

I felt the tin slipping out from underneath my jumper. Thud! It was now lying on the floor at my feet for all the world to see. I was a thief. A hard hand flew across my face which was followed an instant later by a stinging burning pain. My right cheek throbbed and hot tears rolled down my face. The house mother's angry eyes and thunderous voice cut through me as she held my arm in a vice-like grip. "You thief! How dare you take things that don't belong to you. You're nothing but a little tink. Bed for a month. Now get out of my sight!" With my face still smarting from the slap, she shoved me out the door, still yelling and screaming at the top of her voice. "Get out of my sight!" she shouted, over and over.

As I slowly made my way through the playground and out of the home, I knew every step brought me closer to school where yet more humiliation awaited me at cookery class later on in the day. What excuse could I make? I couldn't think of anything.

Then the moment I was dreading all day finally arrived. Mrs Brown gathered all the girls around the large square table at the front of the class, as she always did. Then she asked if everybody had all the ingredients required. Everyone said yes, except me.

Mrs Brown paused for a moment, then looked at me in a strange sort of way. Her eyes were kind and gentle. I wasn't sure what to make of it all. It was as if she was seeing me for the very first time. Instead of asking me what my excuse was this time, she quietly told me to go into the cupboard and collect the ingredients I needed. From that moment onwards, I never had to make up another excuse at cookery class again. Every time I went into the class at the start of the lesson, Mrs Brown already had the ingredients laid out waiting for me, and never asked me for a penny. I served out my month-long punishment without a grumble.

Mixing up all the ingredients together and seeing what the finished result would be was one of the reasons I liked cooking so much. It was a difficult art which I was a long way from mastering. How much I still had to learn became clearer during the final test. Mrs Brown explained we were all to be given a recipe to follow, something we'd made already during the year. She said she would not be helping us and that we musn't ask each other for assistance. If we did, that would be looked upon as cheating and we would fail the test.

As we stood at our tables, she handed each of us a slip of paper telling us what we were going to bake and the list of ingredients required. Written on mine was a recipe for scones. All around me, the rest of the girls were already busy measuring out ingredients into bowls or whisking away madly. They looked confident, like they knew exactly what to do. I felt the very opposite as I stared hard at the piece of paper wondering where to begin.

An hour or so later the test was over and we were told to stop what we were doing. Mrs Brown came round with a clipboard in hand to give us the marks she thought our creations deserved. She stopped beside the first girl, making some very positive comments.

"They look very nice indeed," said an obviously delighted Mrs Brown. "Pretty little jam tarts, well made."

My classmate's face beamed, proud of being complimented so highly. Mrs Brown picked up one of the tarts from the plate and took a small bite.

"Mmmm ... lovely, good texture, nice flavour!"

She put the tart down and wrote a mark on the clipboard. Then she moved on to the next girl who looked rather pleased with herself.

"Very nice," said Mrs Brown, admiring the fairy cakes. "They've risen beautifully." Again, she took the smallest of bites and paused. "They're delicious!" she said enthusiastically.

Mrs Brown continued along the tables giving marks and comments and then it was my turn to be judged. My scones just sat there on the plate for all the world to see, sunken and distinctly green in appearance.

"Ahem …" was Mrs Brown's initial comment. "They look awful. I don't think I'll be tasting them!"

Everyone burst out laughing as she quickly moved on to the next girl. I wasn't disappointed. I didn't blame her at all. My efforts were truly abysmal. I tried my best but I wasn't very good at following instuctions. There was far too much bicarbonate of soda in the scones. Although I liked baking I was no baker as the scones lying on the plate made all too clear. They were not fit for human consumption. Not surprisingly, I failed the test.

I was fortunate, too, having Mrs Brown as my sewing teacher. My sewing was almost as bad as my cooking. Again, even although I enjoyed it very much indeed, I still lacked a lot of the necessary skills. I was extremely good at sewing by hand. Some of the tasks we were given were extremely intricate, but I loved the challenge and found it all so theraputic.

One morning, as we took our usual seats, we noticed Mrs Brown had already laid out a pile of dress and skirt patterns on her big table at the front of the class. She asked us to look through them and decide what we wanted to make. After picking out a pattern for a skirt, Mrs Brown strongly suggested I should make it using a roll of grey coloured material. She was very insistant. I didn't understand it. Grey was so dull. There were many rolls of material sitting on the shelves with colours far more exciting.

After laying the pattern on the cloth and cutting around it, the material was pinned and tacked, ready to be sewn into the finished article. But when Mrs Brown told me to use the electric sewing machine it all turned into a bit of a disaster. The machine kept jamming and Mrs Brown had to keep constantly fixing it. I was struggling to finish the skirt. In the end, Mrs Brown took over and during the next couple of weeks finished it off for me. By then, all the other girls in the class were finished, too. When Mrs Brown asked us to bring in money to pay for the materials, my heart sank. It was easier getting blood out of a stone than money out of the house mother. I tried, even though I knew it was a waste of time. I plucked up the courage but the look on her face said it all. She always dismissed me out of hand.

I asked the house mother for the money for the skirt the following week. Once more, she ignored me completely, packing me off to school without it. This went on for a month, me asking and the house mother refusing, until Mrs Brown put her foot down. She sent the house mother a letter demanding the money and that did the trick. Just before leaving for school, the house mother handed me a sealed envelope. Inside it was the money for the skirt which she told me to hand to the sewing teacher. I was over the moon.

As it turned out, the skirt Mrs Brown made was just right for my school uniform. The colour and style fitted in perfectly and I proudly wore it to school the next day. Mrs Brown saw how my old shabby dirndl skirt made me stand out from the other girls in my class and did something about it. Later, with her help, I went on to make a dress and a pair of pyjamas. Each time the house mother gave me a difficult time, Mrs Brown simply wrote another letter and the money materialised.

At last, I had some modern clothes to wear instead of the old-fashioned cast-offs and hand-me-downs from the second-hand cupboard. A year later, when I walked out the gates of the home for the very last time, I still had them. The skirt and dress and pair of pyjamas were the only decent clothes I owned.

Chapter Ten

I WAS 13 YEARS OF AGE and couldn't tell the time. No one ever made the effort to teach me or think it was something important for me to learn. When anyone asked me to tell them the time, I said something like the big hand was pointing to 12 and the small hand was pointing to two. Little wonder the other kids at the school looked at me as if I was stupid. While in the maths class one afternoon, we were doing sums related to time and I couldn't answer any of the questions. The teacher asked me in front of the whole class if I could read the time. I felt embarrassed.

"No," I admitted, my head hanging in shame.

He told me to go to the back of the class and then never bothered with me after that. Only the bright kids sitting at the front of the class got his full attention. I sat at the back for years and no one ever asked why.

There was no one at the home to help you with homework, and no educational books or materials either. Nobody ever asked if you had any problems at school. You were never encouraged to learn, or to think you could ever achieve anything in life. Every year, my school report card said my head was always in the clouds, or I was a dreamer, or something similar. The report card never contained anything positive. It seemed to confirm the home's view of me.

The house mother's reports to the authorities were just as negative. All I was capable of achieving in life was the role of a domestic
servant, nothing else. The more that people around me gave up on
me, the more I gave up on myself. It wasn't until I was 15 that I
learned how to tell the time. Years later, I discovered I suffered
from a form of number dyslexia.

๑๑

The five beds in the big girls' room were all neatly made up and the
room was empty. Everybody was down at breakfast. I was fed up
and depressed and wasn't in the mood to join them. So I sat on the
steps leading to the small girls' room. No one cared and no one
would miss me if I died. My thoughts were deep and dark and
unhappy. Today was my birthday and I didn't want to live a day
longer. There was nothing to look forward to, no cards or birthday
wishes to mark this day as anything special. It was the same every
year.

I thought of all the ways I could kill myself, picturing the scene
in my head. Tablets sprang to mind, but there was not a single
asprin to be had anywhere in this place. Cutting my wrist was all
but impossible. Everything in the home was made of plastic. There
was not enough privacy to hang myself either. Too many kids.
Someone was bound to save me in the nick of time. The more I
thought about it, the more I started to laugh. There was no escape,
no way out of here. But seeing the funny side brightened up my
mood, so I went down to breakfast.

It was the weekend and I was determined to give myself some
kind of a birthday treat, so I sneaked out of the home with my
cousin Anne. We made our way over to the field opposite the
home, wading through the tall overgrown grass which came up to
our waists. All around us, dandelions grew wild and sticky willows

stuck to our clothes and hair and witchycoos twirled and danced on the warm summer breeze. There was nobody about as Anne and I shouted and laughed at each other across the abandoned field. We were on the hunt for juicy red plump strawberries, long forgotten about and just waiting to be eaten. They were to be found among the run-down disused plots. Men in white tops and trousers were playing bowls on the green a short distance away. They were much too interested in their game to notice Anne and me running about in the field.

I liked Anne. Her hair was short and raven black. She had pearly white teeth which seemed far too big for her small mouth. Her cheeks were pale and her frame thin and wiry, making her appear undernourished and ill looking. But she was full of grit and fun to be with. Her dad came to the home every Sunday to take her out for the afternoon. He was a lovely man, always smartly dressed in a trilby hat and suit. Whenever he saw me looking out from behind the gates he stopped to speak to me. Then he walked away up the driveway and came back down again a minute later with Anne and her brother and sister. One day, he told me Anne was my cousin. He said he was going to speak to the house mother to see if he could take me out for the afternoon, along with his children. But the house mother refused point-blank to give him permission. Anne's dad was also a great piper. The house mother loved all kinds of Scottish music and invited him into her sitting room to play for her one New Year's Eve. I enjoyed listening to him as I lay in bed.

Suddenly, I was back in the field again when Anne let out an almighty scream as she tripped over one of the corrugated tin roofs lying half-buried and hidden in the long grass. There was a large gash running down her leg with blood pouring from it. I panicked, not knowing what to do. Luckily, Anne's frantic screams alerted the men playing bowls. They rushed over to help. One man pulled off his shirt and wrapped it tightly around Anne's leg while another ran off to telephone for an ambulance. As I watched, the shirt gradually changed from white to deep red as it soaked up the blood oozing out from underneath it. By the time the ambulance arrived to take her to hospital, Anne's screams had subsided into sobs. My appetite for strawberries was long gone as I made my way back to the home.

When the house mother found out, I got into such trouble. I was sent to bed straight after tea for a whole month. Anne returned from hospital with stitches in her leg. She also got the same punishment. But at least we had each other to talk to. It was one birthday I would never forget.

The house mother loved to show off her new hats. There was an unspoken competition between her and the ladies of the church we went to every Sunday. The house mother liked to be centre stage. I don't think God approved of their false smiles and greetings and the insincere nods of acknowledgement before and after each service. Heads turned as soon as she entered the church one Sunday wearing a two-piece green tweed suit with a lovely green wide-brimmed hat to match. She spent a fortune on it, but it produced the desired result and made the ladies rather envious.

The long walk to church and the service was part and parcel of the routine at the home and everyone, whether believer or non-believer, had to attend. Agnes hated going because she was an aetheist and often argued her point of view at the dining room table at breakfast time. She was 14 years of age with a mind of her own. This greatly annoyed the house mother who thought it her Christian duty to convert her. The house mother's anger grew in frustration and her face turned redder by the second but Agnes, ever the independent thinker, never backed down. She was too smart and stuck to her guns and always won the argument in the end. I admired her for that.

We all sat in the two rows of pews at the back of the church, pretending to listen to the minister's fire and brimstone sermon. The house mother sat in the middle of us. The sermon dragged on and on, like it always did, week after week. It was supposed to inspire the congregation. But I never understood any of what the minister was saying and my mind quickly switched off.

I found my gaze moving from the hymn book in my hand and lowering to the floor and the smart looking stylish brogues the house mother was wearing. I could almost smell the newness of the leather as I tried to count the number of eyelets through which the brown laces passed. She must have noticed me looking at her shoes, admiring them, but she never said anything at the time or passed any comment.

Back at the home after church one day she said, quite out of the blue, "You like these shoes?"

Puzzled, I replied, "Yes, I really like them."

"Well, I'm getting another pair of shoes and you can have them when I've finished with them."

I could hardly believe it and barely contained the happiness I felt inside me. But it seemed to take for ever until the house mother passed me the brown brogue shoes a few weeks later. I now held them in my hands. Quickly loosening the laces at the front, I slipped my feet into them and they fitted perfectly, my first pair of grown-up shoes. What a day that was. What a feeling. No more old-fashioned badly fitting second-hand cast-offs. I felt I was walking on air. These shoes told the world I was now grown up, never mind they didn't match my three-quarter length grey school socks. I didn't care as I enjoyed listening the next day to the sound of the heels echoing as I walked up and down the school corridor. I wanted the whole world to hear them. When I returned to the home, I put my everyday slippers on and placed the brogues carefully in one of the metal baskets underneath a bench in the cloakroom. They were now ready for school again in the morning.

But my feelings of exhilaration were short lived. After breakfast, I hurried into the cloakroom to get ready for school. My face dropped and my heart sank and I stared in disbelief at my new shoes. They were now on Maggie's feet. Maggie beamed from one end of her face to the other. The house mother stood watching me.

"I've decided to give the shoes to Maggie," she announced. The house mother couldn't disguise the hint of a smirk spreading over her face as she smiled back at me. It was a wicked smile. But there was nothing I could do or say. I knew better than to challenge her decision. Doing so might lead to a slap on the face and being sent to bed after tea for a week or maybe longer. I held back the rising anger and the tears welling up inside me. Maggie walked out the door with her head held high, wearing my beautiful shoes.

For months afterwards, whenever I saw Maggie wearing the shoes to school I was reminded of the hurt I felt that morning. Maggie didn't take care of the shoes. Eventually, she wore them out and they were discarded. I never understood why the house mother gave me the shoes one day, only to take them away the next. She knew how much they meant to me, how I admired them every time she wore them to church on a Sunday. The incident was just one of the many humiliations I suffered over the years. Every one of them hurt me deeply and only added to the hatred and resentment I felt.

☙❧

The sky was cloudy and overcast with rain threatening. It wasn't the best of days to go to the beach. But the staff at the home wanted us away and out from under their feet, so we had to go whether we liked it or not. This was quite usual during the school summer holidays. It was also a cheap way to keep us amused. All it cost was a few dried-up jam sandwiches and some diluted juice. Providing sandwiches and juice also meant they didn't have to cook us an evening meal when we returned.

I couldn't see my brown swimming costume anywhere, even though I rummaged through the chest of drawers by the window a dozen times.

"Bloody thing!"

Anne rarely swore, which was why I turned around. She was all in a fluster, trying to stretch her bikini top over boobs grown a size bigger since the last time she wore it. But, try as she might, it wouldn't stretch far enough. "Stupid bloody thing. I can't wear that!" she cried out, throwing it angrily onto her neatly made bed.

I never answered her or made any comment. Instead, I carried on hunting for my swimming costume. Anne was muttering under her breath all the while. At last I found it, and with swimming costume in hand, made my way to the door.

"Patsy," said Anne, rather sheepishly.

I knew what was coming.

"You're about the same height as me," she continued. "Why don't we do a swap?"

"No way!" I said, emphatically. My figure was developing nicely but my boobs were not yet as big as Anne's. Although I looked good, I was shy and very self-conscious and wearing a bikini would be like baring my soul. I wasn't ready for that, or so I thought.

Anne was persistent if nothing else. She was determined to have my swimsuit, no matter what my objections were. So I gave in, reluctantly. I felt sorry for her. Anne loved swimming and would be unable to do so without my swimsuit. At least that's what I told myself.

Within half an hour we were at the beach, running in and out of the sand dunes until we found the perfect spot. The children quickly tore off their clothes, eager to get to the water's edge. But I held back, undressing slowly and folding my clothes carefully before placing them on the sand. I was playing for time, building up the courage to face a beach packed with holidaymakers dressed in a bikini. This was madness. I was going to be stared at, or laughed at. But all the time, I was heading inch by embarrassing inch towards the safety and privacy of the gently lapping waves.

The water was freezing but no one seemed to notice but me. All around, children young and old were laughing and kicking up the water with their feet, splashing each other and having great fun. Further up the beach, tiny tots with buckets and spades were building sandcastles or burying themselves in sand with mums and dads watching approvingly. As I walked further out, I started to get used to the cold water now lapping my thighs. I immersed myself fully and began to swim away from the shoreline, pushing the calm water with my hands, watching the ripples moving gently outwards with every stroke. Except for the company of the odd gull hovering on the breeze, I was alone in the stillness and tranquillity which was taking me far from the sounds of children screaming on the beach.

But I was heading towards danger without realising it. My senses hardly registered the growing strength of the current which was now pulling me towards the distant line of wooden barriers. The barriers were built to protect swimmers from strong tides and currents. All of a sudden, my mind was filled with blind panic when I realised I was caught in the grip of an unseen undercurrent. I was heading towards the centre of a swirling vortex which was trying to suck me under. Time stood still. I fought and struggled and kicked out. But I couldn't break the power holding me, sapping my strength, dragging me deeper into the watery grave now drawing closer with every precious breath and mouthful of salt water. The situation was hopeless. I was resigned to my fate. I was going to die.

Barely aware of the strong arms now grasping my waist, all I could see through the watery film covering my eyes was the circular swirl of sand at the bottom of the murky depths. Suddenly, I gasped in lungfuls of pure sweet air and daylight replaced the blackness of a moment before. Somehow, I was at the water's edge but had no idea how I got there. I was alone. There was nobody beside me. My thighs and legs were covered in blood from dozens of scratches. I was crying from shock. One or two holidaymakers came over and asked me if I was OK. They wanted to know what had happened but I felt too dazed to talk to them.

Slowly, I walked up the beach to the promenade where the first aid hut was situated. The blood and sand was washed off and revealed only superficial injuries. A short while later, I felt calm enough to join Anne and the rest of the children playing on the beach. No one mentioned my cuts and grazes so I never told them anything. There was no point because I might have got into trouble.

I never found out who saved me. It was a real mystery. Although the events played over in my mind for days on end, I still couldn't figure it out. Even if I had cried out for help, I was too far out for anyone to hear me. One moment I was fighting to stay alive and the next, walking alone at the water's edge. It was a puzzle I've not been able to explain, even to this day.

☙❧

If summer meant long days spent playing on the beach, winter was all about freezing winds and ice and snow and rain chilling us to the bone. Wellington boots and shoes, which had long seen better days, barely kept out the cold or the slush and rain. Feet were left soaking wet. The half darkness of early morning only added to the misery as we trudged the mile or so to school. The route took us through the long narrow streets of Old Aberdeen, past Aberdeen University's King's College and the church with its old high stone wall where William Wallace's hand was supposed to be buried.

During my first year at high school, I always dreaded passing the wall. I really believed the stories that Wallace's hand sometimes appeared and grabbed people passing by. So I held my breath and ran past the spot, fully expecting the hand to emerge and stop me dead in my tracks.

Without warning, our routine was changed. Instead of hanging about the school playground after lunch, we were ordered to walk back to the home. We stayed in the playroom for about twenty minutes and then walked all the way back to school again for afternoon lessons. It just added to the misery. We were not allowed to leave the freezing playroom to warm ourselves inside the home. Only the house mother's favourites were allowed to. We stamped up and down to feel our feet or blew air into our hands to generate some heat. It was the only way to coax life into wet and frozen limbs. Answering the call of nature meant walking outside, past the side of the home to an old outside toilet block. From there, you sometimes caught sight of the house mother or one of her favourites through the kitchen window, standing at the stone sink washing up the dinner dishes. So many times I longed to be invited inside, just to stand for a few minutes in front of the roaring fire which I knew was in the kitchen. If the house mother caught you looking in, she chased you away with an angry dismissive wave of her arm.

Even when some of the children developed painful chilblains on their feet and hands, which happened regularly in winter, she showed little or no sympathy. They were left to get on with it. Sometimes the tears rolled down their faces as they walked to school. Some decent waterproof footwear and heating in the play-room was all it would have taken to make life a little better for us all. But that never happened. So we suffered, in silence, winter after winter.

Chapter Eleven

GREEN SHOOTS WERE SPRINGING up rapidly everywhere, marking the end of a very long winter. We were longing for better weather after being stuck in for months on end with only school and church on a Sunday morning to break the dreary monotony of life in the home. I was 14 and craving excitement, something different in my life, anything to save me from the boredom which was slowly driving me mad. So it was a huge surprise when the house mother made a sudden announcement at teatime. Children who had no family to take them out at weekends were to go on a day trip.

One by one, the house mother called out the names of the children who were going. I felt a sudden rush of excitement at the prospect of escaping the drudgery, if only for a few hours. This was what I was waiting for, praying for, and now my prayers were answered. It seemed like an age until the moment the house mother called out my name. My heart leapt. Now it was official. Thank you God!

The trip was the one and only topic of conversation over the coming weeks. The house mother cranked up the anticipation with cryptic hints and clues, but never actually told us where we were going. As a result, all sorts of exotic destinations were suggested and then discarded as imaginations ran riot and rumours abounded. We were just going to have to wait patiently for the big day, whenever that might be.

At last, the announcement finally came one Saturday evening, when we were sitting down for tea at the dining room table. The younger children squealed out in delight as the house mother once more called out their names. But she forgot to call out mine. It was a temporary mistake, nothing more.

"The van will be coming tomorow morning," the house mother continued. "We'll be leaving at 10."

A cheer went up. Some children clapped their hands. They were so happy. Then the house mother suddenly pointed a finger at me.

"You will not be going!"

Her words didn't quite register for a moment, even though I heard every syllable clearly. I was not going on the trip? Was that what she said? A black cloud of disappointment descended over me, swirling like a vortex, blocking everything out and sucking me in. Why not? What have I done? Am I being punished? The house mother turned away from the devastation written all over my face.

The events of the day flashed through my mind. I searched hard for something, anything I may have done wrong but maybe wasn't aware of. But there was nothing. Perhaps it was yesterday, or the day before, a wrong word somewhere, a remark which caused some offence? Maybe my shoes were dirty? What did I do that was so wrong? There was no answer. Everywhere I looked there were smiling faces and the buzz of anticipation was almost electric. In contrast, I felt rejected, deflated, alone in the middle of an ocean of excitement. I turned my back on it all and went to bed.

The big day arrived and breakfast disappeared in record time. A flurry of activity followed upstairs with everyone rushing about to get ready for the arrival of the van. I was banished to the playground, which was declared out of bounds to the rest of the children now dressed in their Sunday best. As the van appeared in the driveway and made its way to the front door, I still harboured the faintest of hope the house mother might take pity on me and change her mind, even at this late stage. So I stood in the playground in full view as everyone jumped into the van under her watchful gaze.

The house mother was in her element, supervising where everybody sat in the van, barking out orders like some trumped-up army general. But never once did she turn and look towards me, even though she couldn't help but see me standing alone, looking to the world like the original Orphan Annie. But I failed to move her. She slammed the sliding doors shut and a few seconds later, the van sailed past me down the driveway and out of sight. As the silence decended, I realised I was on my own, the only one left in the home.

It was a long and a sad day for me. I tried to amuse myself in the large empty playground. Occasionally, I caught a glimpse of a member of staff through the kitchen window. But no one checked on me to see if I was all right. The hours dragged by. I wandered up and down aimlessly, still trying to work out what it was I did wrong. The house mother never told me and I still wondered, years later.

I was sitting eating my tea when the van returned and everyone piled into the dining room, happy and still excited by their day out in the country. Some of the younger children were hot and sweaty and completely worn out from all the running about. Everyone enjoyed the day but I didn't want to know anything about it. I didn't want to be reminded of all the fun I missed. The anger was still inside me and so was the disappointment and hurt.

The house mother ignored me completely and walked by me through to the kitchen to have tea. As I watched her back disappear through the kitchen door, my resentment of her grew only deeper. Someday, I swore to myself, there would be a day of reckoning, not too far distant, when I would have the power over my life and not this cruel and calculating excuse for a woman. That day was surely coming, very soon, and I couldn't wait.

◈

I never really minded going to the beach, even during the Easter break when it was still quite chilly. But sometimes the day felt really long when the weather was dull and rainy. I was feeling particularly bored at the end of one such day and decided to go alone up Broad Hill instead of passing it by as we usually did on the way back to the home. The steep hill was always a favourite haunt of local children who made improvised sledges from large pieces of discarded cardboard which they usually found lying outside the shops in the area. They spent all day having great fun racing up the 100-foot-high hill and then sliding down its steep slopes.

Broad Hill was really a long low ridge running parallel with the Kings Links golf course and the shoreline beyond. After climbing to the top, I picked up the path which runs its whole length and was soon lost in deep thoughts, enjoying the solitude and the spectacular view of the sea stretching to the distant horizon.

I don't quite know when I first noticed the three teenage lads sitting a few feet from the edge of the path, some way up ahead of me. But, as I drew closer, there was something about them that made me feel uncomfortable. Maybe it was the way they were talking to each other in whispers. I knew I just wanted to get past them as quickly as possible. They looked red in the face and sweaty and cardboard sledges lay on the ground beside them. I assumed they'd been sliding down the hill and were now resting.

The oldest of the group, who was aged about 17, suddenly shouted out to his mates, "I fancy a good ride."

Instantly I knew I was in deep trouble, vulnerable, alone. Fear gripped my whole body. My legs turned to lead weights.

"Let's pull her knickers down."

I looked straight ahead, into the distance, trying hard to control the rising panic. My heart thumped in my head. I was scared. My pace quickened. But before I knew what was happening, the three of them formed a circle around me, barring my way, fingers touching and tugging at my cardigan as they tried to pull it off. I begged them to stop, but they ignored me. Tears filled my eyes. Time stood still. No one would hear my screams, and they knew it. They all laughed aloud as one of them triumphantly swung my cardigan in the air, like it was some sporting trophy or prize. As he did so, he egged on the others who were now pawing and tearing at my T-shirt. I gripped it tightly, fighting back with every bit of strength I could muster. But I felt defenceless. This was a one-sided contest I knew I would lose.

"Stop!" a voice boomed out from nowhere.

It stopped them dead in their tracks. As they stood motionless, not knowing what to do next, their grip on me loosened.

"Let her go, now!"

The young lads instantly obeyed the smartly dressed man standing just a few feet away from us. He was tall and broad and dressed in a grey pin-striped suit.

"Clear off!" he shouted in an angry threatening voice.

The boys knew there was no messing with him and high-tailed it over the other side of the hill, disappearing out of sight.

"Are you OK lass?" said the stranger in a kind and caring voice.

"Yes," I sobbed quietly.

My voice sounded shaky and my legs felt wobbly. He picked up my cardigan which was lying in a crumpled heap on the ground.

"I'll walk you down the hill," he said.

When we reached the end of the path, the stranger patted me

gently on the back, reassuring me I was safe and that it was best I got myself straight home. I walked a few yards on. When I turned to wave goodbye, there was no one there. I looked all around me but the stranger was gone, vanished, as if he had never been. I couldn't believe it.

Walking the long road home, I tried to make sense of it all. I knew I would never feel safe going up Broad Hill again. It was a valuable lesson. I was 14 and had just experienced an uglier side of life outside the protective bubble of the home. It frightened me. While I never spoke about the incident to anyone, I was thankful someone had appeared at the right time and at the right place, saving me from being seriously assaulted or even worse.

I never found out who the stranger was. But I still think of him, even after so many years have passed. Where did he come from? Where did he go? The area was very open. There was nowhere to hide. Anyone walking on the hill was easily seen for miles. Yet, I never saw anyone coming. Neither did the young lads. It was yet another mystery.

ॐ

Louise was small and slim with fair shoulder-length wavy hair, who spoke little and never drew much attention to herself. She was a classmate, but not a friend, for I never made any at high school. I tried my best to make friends. I really wanted to make friends, to be just like the rest of my classmates, but it was hopeless. My existence was so strictly controlled by rules which governed every tiny aspect of daily life, from the moment I got up each day to when I went to bed at night; this made it too difficult to develop any personal friendships. Early one evening, while I was watching television in the television room with the rest of the children in the home, a member of staff came through and told me to go to the house mother's sitting room. I was surprised, and a little apprehensive, immediately thinking I must have done something wrong. Unless you were one of the house mother's favourites, the sitting room was out of bounds.

I was 10 years of age when I was last invited in there. That was four years ago. It was the time I switched on the Christmas lights. I rememembered squatting on my knees on a thick deep-piled Axminster carpet and being told to wave like the Queen, over and over again, until my arms ached and the movement was perfect. The house mother was determined I was not going to show her up.

Many times since then, as I passed the sitting room door, I wanted to knock but was too afraid of the consequences of doing so. I stood there, with hand raised, but always courage failed me at the last second. So I turned away, keeping my problems and difficulties to myself. But this felt different. What was it she wanted of me? What did I do wrong today? I couldn't think of anything. As I approached the sitting room door, the house mother was standing half in and half out. She looked sternly at me.

In a sharp raised voice, she said, "There's someone called Louise on the telephone for you. She wants to know if you can come out or if she can come and see you. You tell her you can't and not to call this number again."

The house mother pointed me towards the hallway telephone sitting on a table at the main entrance to the home. The receiver was off the hook and I picked it up. I said nothing to Louise other than what the house mother told me to say and hung up. That was the end of my first ever telephone call.

All the while, the house mother listened intently to make sure I said exactly what she told me to say. Then she questioned me. I felt like a criminal. "Did you tell her to call you? Did you give her the home's number?" she asked accusingly.

I stammered out, "No, I told her nothing. I don't know how she got the number."

The house mother looked long and hard, almost searching into my very soul, not convinced by my nervous reply. Then, with the well-practised dismissive gesture she always used, she waved me away without a further word.

Quickly, I walked back through to the television room, glad to be out of the house mother's view. All through the rest of the evening, my thoughts kept returning to the telephone call and how and why Louise had tried to contact me. I longed to have a friend, to do all the things other teenagers did, like going to discos or youth clubs or just visiting each other's house to listen to records and talk about boyfriends and clothes. But I knew all of that was impossible.

Next day, at school, Louise kept her distance and I felt too uncomfortable to say anything. How I wished I could have explained I didn't deliberately shun her. But I had no choice. I had to do what I was told. I was never allowed to do normal things, like other girls my age. I think Louise felt as empty as I was inside. She was struggling to cope with the death of her father, a fisherman, who was lost at sea. So most days she sat quietly in class, withdrawn, never laughing or joining in. Perhaps the telephone call was a cry for help, the beginning of her reaching out. Maybe, when she saw the sadness in me, she recognised it in herself and making friends with me was a first step. It must have taken a lot for her to pick up the telephone. Then I cut her dead. She never called the home again. We never became friends.

❦

Louise reminded me so much of Jennifer. Years before, when I was looking through the steel bars of the playground fence, I noticed a young girl aged about 10 being led by the hand up the gravel drive-way to the front door. The lady holding her hand was dishevelled in appearance and her once stylish hair now showed the last remnants of a perm. The lady noticed me and smiled self-consciously as if to hide the large buck teeth protruding out from her mouth and continued walking past me up the driveway. She hesitated for a moment or two just a few steps away from the door, as if unsure what to do next, and then rang the doorbell.

After some words were exchanged, the two of them entered the home. I continued playing for a short while until it was time to come in. The girl I saw earlier was now sitting in the dining room. I was told her name was Jennifer and that she had come to live with us. Jennifer's hair was soft and short and dark. One eye squinted as she looked at you. She was very shy and withdrawn and hardly said a word. All she did was stare at the floor. We were told the following morning she wasn't coming to school with us. Instead, she was going to a school for children they called "back-ward". Jennifer was a good few years older than me. Like me, she never had any family visits over the years. She never played much with the rest of us, always preferring her own company. I learned much later the lady with the buck teeth, who I never saw again, was her mother.

Some five years down the road, it was time for Jennifer to get a job. So she found herself employed at a nearby woollen mill which made jumpers and knitted hats and gloves. But after only a few days Jennifer was in floods of tears in the kitchen, talking to the house mother, when she was supposed to be at work. I was hanging around the home killing time, prior to a visit to the dentist.

"You've been fired after only a few days at the job!" I heard the house mother shout out.

The anger in her voice only made Jennifer cry and sob all the more as she tried her best to explain. But the house mother was having none of it. "So what are you going to do now?" she demanded. "If you can't do a simple job like that then you're no good to anyone."

I tiptoed out the kitchen, frightened of the house mother turning her anger on me, and thankfully made my way to the dentist. The next time I saw Jennifer, she was carrying her belongings and clothes from the big girls' room, where we both slept, to an adjoining room used for members of staff. I realised Jennifer now had a new job, looking after us. It was not unknown for children in the home to end up being employed as members of staff. As I found out later, Jennifer was the replacement for another staff member who was once brought up in the home and who had now been thrown out.

It all happened just a few days earlier. The house mother was tipped off and burst into the girl's room in the middle of the night, catching her in bed with her boyfriend. So she was dismissed on the spot. The shouting and swearing woke me up. I heard the house mother tell her to pack her bags and get out. The nightime visits had been going on for quite some time. The boyfriend climbed up the drainpipe on the outside wall and entered the room through an open window. Then he sneaked back down the drainpipe in the early hours before anyone in the home stirred. But the dismissal left the house mother short staffed and Jennifer conveniently filled the gap.

Jennifer, not being very bright, struggled with every task she was given. The house mother lacked patience at the best of times and hated any sloppiness or excuses. So she was always on Jennifer's back, shouting constantly and taking her bad temper out on her. She thought nothing of barging into Jennifer's room at three o'clock in the morning, cursing and swearing and dragging her by the hair out of bed, hitting her about the head and bundling her down the stairs half naked because she forgot to blacken the kitchen stove. I saw it all, peeking out from underneath the blankets. My bed looked directly into Jennifer's room. She was terrified as she raised her arms above her head in an effort to protect herself.

I felt powerless to help. I could do nothing but watch as the house mother's anger grew day by day and Jennifer turned more and more into a skivvy. It was nothing for Jennifer to begin working at 6 o'clock on a freezing morning and still be slaving away late into the night, long after we were all in bed.

I am ashamed to say the house mother's attitude also rubbed off on the rest of us as we blamed Jennifer for everything we did wrong. Of course, we were simply saving our own skins, not realising how wrong it was getting her into so much trouble. It just became part of everyday life. But Jennifer was never vindictive or angry with any of us. She had sympathy for the children she grew up with and never told tales on anyone. I liked her a lot. She was a gentle soul who deserved so much better. But there was no home to call her own or anyone to care. So she had no option but to stick it out, for years and years. She was the Cinderella and the house mother was the wicked stepmother.

Chapter Twelve

As I put my new swimming costume on in the changing rooms, a tingle of excitement ran through me. I was more than a little nervous, too, although determined not to show it. All would be decided soon, I reassured myself, as I made my way from the changing rooms with the rest of my team mates a few moments later and walked slowly up to the top of the swimming pool and the starting blocks. There was hardly an empty seat anywhere. I looked around me at all the faces staring down, expectant, anticipating the start of the relay race.

"Ready, set, go!" said the starter, firing his starting gun.

A sharp crack split the air and the race was on. The girl leading our team was quickest diving into the brightly lit pool. Within seconds, she was pulling ahead of the rest of the field. The race was the highlight of the inter-school championships. I was picked for the team because I was considered a good swimmer. We practised hard for weeks, even going to the pool during some Saturdays, so determined were we all to win. Now the hard work was paying off. Everything was going to plan.

It was during one of these Saturdays I happened to accidentally catch the eye of a young lad at the other end of the noisy crowded pool. There was something about him as he stood there with two other boys, both around the same age. I kept looking at him. He kept staring back at me. Suddenly, I knew he was my brother. I couldn't explain how I knew. But the feeling inside was so powerful, so overwhelming. I looked carefully at the other two boys with him. Yes, I was certain. They were also my brothers. There was no doubt in my mind. But they didn't notice me. The spell was broken in the next instant when they were all ushered out of the pool by an elderly man. I felt sad as I watched them disappear out of sight.

I discovered years later they were indeed my brothers, Michael, Andy and Alec. But no one ever told me. I never knew they existed. It felt strange, meeting them for the very first time at the children's home they were brought up in. I was 19, with a child of my own, and I recognised them instantly. They were the three young lads I saw at the other end of the pool many years before.

We were way out in front as the second girl in our team of three dived into the water, increasing the lead yet further with every stroke. Then it was my turn. After diving in confidently, I swam powerfully in my hand-knitted costume which was given to me the night before by the house mother. I was determined to increase the gap between me and the swimmer in second place who was by now some five or six yards behind. The crowd included children from the home and many pupils from my school with their parents. They all screamed and cheered me on, sensing victory would soon be ours.

I was punching through the water as fast as I could. Suddenly, I felt the weight of the water pulling my swimming costume down the front of my chest. At first, I tried to ignore it. I touched the end of the pool and pushed off to swim the final length. But with every yard I swam, the baggier the swimming costume became. By the time I reached the middle of the pool, it had slipped all the way down to my waist and was gathered around my stomach in a shapeless mass.

It could only happen to me. Horrified, I stretched and pulled at the costume while still vainly trying to swim. At the same time, I was desperately attempting to preserve my dignity which was disappearing fast. But all eyes in the gallery were transfixed by the unfolding scene. They missed none of the detail as they got an unexpected eyeful of my well-formed breasts. At that moment, the second placed swimmer swam past me, and then the third, and before I knew it, I was the only person left in the pool. I felt a thousand eyes following my every movement as I struggled to walk through the water while holding the costume up with both hands. It was a long lonely embarrassing walk back to the edge of the pool.

As I slowly climbed up the steps to get out, the costume stretched so much it was now completely see through. My embarrassment was complete. I made a mad dash to the changing rooms where I found my team mates waiting. But they were far from disappointed with me, as I expected. Although I lost them the race, it didn't matter. They had never laughed so much in their lives.

When I returned to the home later that evening I felt so annoyed we lost the race, and angry at being given such an inappropriate costume for such a public event. Unsurprisingly, I was the only one not to see the funny side of things. It took me weeks to get over the embarrassment and years to look back at it all and laugh. It really was so funny.

၈⃝၈

It was coming up to the summer holidays and my fifteenth birthday passed by unnoticed as usual. Sitting down at the dining room table finishing my tea with the rest of the children, I tried to pluck up the courage to tell the house mother I wanted to leave the home for good. I didn't want to live here a day longer than I had to.

The house mother sat eating at her table in the middle of the room. She barely moved and almost blended with the furniture and fittings. Only her eyes blinked and darted to and fro, watching everything going on around her. For as long as I remembered, she always sat that way, looming over us all to make sure nothing passed her by.

"When can I leave?" I finally blurted out.

I did it. I've said the words. For the first time in a long time, I managed to get her attention. The expression on the house mother's face turned first to shock and then to anger.

"You ..." She looked stunned. Her voice trailed away and was followed by a sharp intake of breath. "You should be grateful for everything I've done for you!", she finally said in a low, hissing, venomous voice.

But her hate-filled words simply washed over me for I knew there was very little she could do to stop me leaving. I was at the age where she couldn't wield her authority over me any more, or threaten or intimidate me. Then she stopped herself short, as if realising the situation had changed and further words were now useless. The balance of power was shifting, for ever, and she knew she no longer had control.

In a calm voice, she said, "I'll make arrangements."

That was it. I couldn't believe what I was hearing. For the first time I felt empowered, not scared, not frightened, triumphant. It was the greatest feeling ever. The weight that always seemed to be on top of me, smothering me, pressing me down for years, was now lifted as if by magic. My life was about to change. I felt as light as a feather. As I made my way out of the dining room, I couldn't wait for my day of freedom to arrive.

Lying in my bed that night I felt very happy, but the feeling was tinged with sadness at the thought of leaving the rest of the children at the home behind. I tried to remember the faces of all those who'd come and gone over the years, wondering if everything had worked out for them in the big wide world. I thought about the old house mother who died and reflected on the fateful day I first laid eyes on the woman walking up the driveway who shortly afterwards became the present house mother.

❦

It was now my final day at high school. The last two weeks were agony, every hour feeling like it was two and each day dragging by almost in slow motion. But now, here I was at the very last assembly, and my name was being called out. I walked up on to the stage in front of the whole school to collect my Red Cross certificate in childcare. It had taken me two years of study and a two-hour written exam to gain the certificate. Proudly, I accepted it from the headmaster. It was my one and only achievement.

The childcare classes were held once a week, mostly at the school but occasionally at a nearby medical centre. It was there I saw rows and rows of jars containing foetuses floating in preserving fluid. They were all at different stages of development. I was shocked the first time I saw them. Then, as we sat among them learning how to knit baby booties, I was saddened to think none had made it into the world.

The school bell rang and marked the end of my schooldays. I made my way outside and into the playground. Some of the boys from my class were laughing and messing about. They played a farewell prank on the teachers, letting the air out of their car tyres. I enjoyed walking out the school gates for the very last time, glad to be leaving so many unhappy memories behind me. Schooldays were supposed to be the best days of your life, but not for me. They were difficult years, often humiliating, a real waste of time in the end.

The following Monday morning, the house mother told me to go down to the Labour Exchange and get a job. But I had no idea what the Labour Exchange was or even how to get there. She told me to take a bus into town but gave me no instructions as to what bus to take, how to find it, or where the bus stop was. What was I supposed to say to the bus conductor? How much money did I have to hand over? No one ever bothered to tell me how you caught a bus, not in all my years at the home. We never went on buses. We walked everywhere. The only buses I knew were the ones the church laid on to take us to the annual Sunday school picnics. This was a whole new world opening up to me and I had no idea what to do. The house mother disappeared out for the morning after handing me some money and just left me to get on with it.

I walked down the driveway feeling nervous and apprehensive, worrying about the task ahead of me. Outside, standing alone trying to get my bearings, I noticed a lady across the road weighed down with heavy bags of shopping.

"Excuse me!" I shouted out. "Where do you get a bus to the Labour Exchange?"

She paused to think for a moment then reeled off a string of directions and instructions. She may as well have saved her breath. It was all too much to take in. The only parts I remembered were "city centre bus" and that the bus stop was on the same side of the road as I was already on. I thanked her anyway.

The people waiting at the bus stop looked so natural and calm compared to me. I felt flustered and sweaty and my heart was racing. But I didn't want to show myself up. So I stood just like they did, pretending not to have a care in the world, acting as if I'd caught the bus hundreds of times before. It wasn't long before a bus appeared and I got on. The bus conductor knew instantly I didn't have a clue where I was going. "I'll give you a nod when it's time to get off," he suggested.

He was so kind and I felt much happier and relaxed now as I slowly counted out the correct fare and handed it over. I could hardly believe I was actually managing to take a bus all on my own. It was a great feeling. I felt so grown up. After about twenty minutes or so, the bus arrived at the city centre. The bus conductor gave me the nod he said he would and I got off. In front of me was the sign for the Labour Exchange and I walked through the front door.

A middle-aged lady sat at a large desk on which lay a bundle of papers next to a black telephone. The room was grey and drab looking and sparsely decorated. I noticed the single filing cabinet standing against the wall behind her. The lady looked at me. "Can I help you?" she said, peering through half spectacles which highlighted the rather big bump on the bridge of her nose.

"I'm looking for a job," I replied, nervously.

"Take a seat." Her voice was sharp and commanding. She pointed lazily to the empty seat at the front of her desk. "So what sort of job are you looking for?"

"I'm not sure," I replied.

"Have you had any experience?"

"What do you mean?"

"Working!"

"No," I said.

I felt a bit silly. The lady looked at me with an annoyed expression on her face. This wasn't the sort of interview she needed first thing on a Monday morning. She thumbed through the pile of documents on her desk and pulled out a single sheet of paper and looked at it carefully. I watched her eyes scanning from left to right and then up and down. "There's a job going at the Harbour

Bar. They're looking for a barmaid," she said, shoving the piece of paper in my hand. "It's £3 a week, live in. The address is on the paper."

The door opened and someone else walked in.

"Can I help you?" she said, completely ignoring me now.

I took the hint and was off the seat and out the door on my way to catch the bus home. A short while later, I stood in the kitchen rather pleased with myself, having achieved what I set out to do. I had a real job. Although the house mother was there, she didn't look at me or make any eye contact. She ignored me and left the kitchen. Eventually, a member of staff asked me how I got on at the Labour Exchange. I showed her the piece of paper with all the details on it. She seemed pleased for me. But I wasn't so sure I could be a barmaid, although I felt excited at the prospect of the job. Whether I would be suitable at all was another question. My mind was filled with doubts.

Later, as we all sat down to tea, the house mother asked me in a sarcastic tone, "Well, what job did you get?"

"I've got an interview as a barmaid."

"Where about is this job?"

"At the Harbour Bar," I replied.

The house mother burst out laughing. I was taken aback by her reaction. It wasn't what I was expecting. I didn't see what was so funny. Then, after composing herself, she looked hard at me. "Don't you know? That's a job for a prostitute. You want to work at the harbour, where all the prostitutes go?"

I didn't know what a prostitute was or what they did. I didn't understand what the house mother was trying to say to me.

"We'll telephone them tomorrow, shall we?"

I sat eating my tea in silence. The house mother said nothing more. My cheeks felt hot and flushed and I felt embarrassed. I kept thinking of the word prostitute. The house mother had used it for years, always reminding me I would grow up to be a prostitute, just like my mother. It was an ugly sounding word. I felt dirty.

The house mother must have thought about it all and then had a change of heart. Next morning, in the kitchen, she told me to get ready and go down to the Labour Exchange again. She had already telephoned them and insisted I was given a more suitable job. They were now expecting me. This time there was no problem finding my way back there. The same lady was sitting at the same desk and recognised me when I walked in.

"It's you again," she said. "Didn't I see you yesterday and give you a job to go to today?"

"Yes, but the lady at Rosehill telephoned you?"

She looked at me blankly, expecting me to say something else.

"The job wasn't suitable," I said.

The lady dipped into the pile of papers once more and pulled out a job for a nanny and handed it to me. "It's live in," she said curtly. "Three boys. Take that with you and telephone the lady. Her name and telephone number are on there along with the address."

The house mother was in the dining room when I got back to the home. She was giving Jennifer a hard time for not taking the polish off the floor properly. "Over there you stupid girl! Don't do it like that."

Poor Jennifer. She never matched up to the standards of cleanliness demanded by the house mother. The more the house mother shouted at her the more mistakes she made. The house mother turned her attention towards me. "Well, what job did they give you this time?" Jennifer was glad of the reprieve.

"It's a job as a nanny," I said, handing over the piece of paper with the employer's details on it.

She slipped the paper into her apron pocket and got back to the business of sorting Jennifer out. Later on in the day, the house

mother told me to get myself tidied up. She telephoned the
number and arranged an interview for the nanny job. The lady was
expecting me around teatime. The house mother handed me back
the paper with the details on. The lady lived in Westburn Road and
an hour or so later I was sitting on a bus heading there. By now, I
was really getting the hang of buses.

Eventually, the bus entered a rather smart area of Aberdeen and
I got off. Westburn Road, which lay only a short distance away, was
a long, steep road. I was suddenly struck by how quiet it was. There
was very little noise or traffic. Tall trees and large mansions stood
either side of me as I walked along, enjoying the sound of birds
singing. The sounds seemed to fill the air. It was a beautiful
evening.

I stumbled across the address I was looking for more by luck
than anything else and walked up the long driveway to the front
door, which was open. The house was grand and imposing. Its
granite walls sparkled in the low evening sunlight. Somebody very
rich lived here, I thought, as I nervously pressed the doorbell at
the side of the door. From somewhere far inside, I listened to the
faint sound of a bell ringing in response.

A slim and rather aloof lady came to the door a few seconds
later. She had a very posh voice and asked me to follow her
through to the drawing room. The lady was smart but casually
dressed with short blonde hair and appeared to be in her middle
thirties. The drawing room was dimly lit with oil paintings
hanging on the walls. Two large leather easy chairs cosied up next
to a roaring fire in the grate. The flickering flames provided most
of the light in the room. Heavy velvet drapes hung from a large
window and prevented daylight from entering. My feet sank into
the deep Axminster rug covering the wooden floor as she invited
me to take a seat.

After formally introducing herself, Mrs Cameron told me she

knew all about my background after talking with the house mother on the telephone. She wanted to see my childcare certificate. "You have brought it?" she said.

"Yes. Here it is."

After satisfying herself it was genuine, Mrs Cameron went on to tell me about her three sons. They were staying at the moment at their grandmother's home. If I wanted the job, I would have to move to Arbroath where she and her husband had just bought a new hotel. The job would not officially begin until the move, which was at the end of the month. In the meantime, would I be willing to help her here, with some of the domestic chores, so she could get on with the packing?

"Yes," I said.

I could see something was troubling her.

"You won't be keeping in touch or visiting your mother, will you?"

"No," I replied, rather puzzled.

She shook my hand and showed me to the front door. I was to start my new job on Monday, 9 a.m. sharp.

Chapter Thirteen

ALL WEEKEND, I thought of nothing else but my new job. I was looking forward to the challenge and to moving away to start my new life. The routine of the home carried on as usual. But as Saturday turned into Sunday, I began to feel less and less a part of it all.

I arrived at Westburn Road exactly on time, as instructed. The boys were still at their grandmother's house. I was looking forward so much to meeting them. Mrs Cameron told me their father was still sorting things out at the new hotel, to make it ready for the end of the month. In the meantime, she was supervising the removal men who were in the process of packing up the family possessions.

My first task was the laundry. Mrs Cameron asked me to follow her outside to the back garden. She led me down some steps into an underground room which was once an old air raid shelter. It was now being used as a laundry room. The room felt cold with its grey stone floor and whitewashed walls. It was perfect for storing the jars of home-made jam and other preserves filling several rows of shelves. In the far corner stood a modern looking washing machine. Mrs Cameron quickly showed me how to use it and then left me to get on with washing a large pile of towels and clothes belonging to the family.

Several hours later, the washing was finished. The clothes were pegged out and hanging on the washing line. After reporting back to Mrs Cameron, I was told to start dusting. The house was enormous, which I didn't fully appreciate at the time of my interview. Now I realised it was more like a mansion. There were still many expensive ornaments and paintings around the place waiting to be packed away, so I was rather nervous. I didn't want to break anything.

Mrs Cameron sent me into the large kitchen to wash up the leftover plates from lunch. When I finished them, and then cleaned and tidied up some more, the day was over. It was time to make my way homewards. I was pleased enough by the way I coped on my first day at the job, even although I felt far from confident at times.

The rest of the week carried on in much the same way. I followed Mrs Cameron's instructions to the letter, never giving her cause for any complaint or concern. But it was difficult to relax in her company. Even although she made the effort to be friendly and to put me at my ease, I still felt anxious and nervous talking to her, and inferior. We were classes apart. She was a woman with money and position, surrounded by luxury and wealth, while I came from the lowliest of backgrounds.

I met Mr Cameron for the first time on the Friday. He spoke with a posh accent and struck me as a well-educated man. Slim and of average height, with black hair, Mr Cameron found it difficult to relax or to concentrate on the matter in hand. Instead, his mind appeared preoccupied all the time, as if filled with worries and concerns.

The boys were now staying at their grandmother's home until the move, he informed me. It was easier that way, he said. Looking after two lively young boys and a baby was much too difficult given all the packing and organisation which still had to be done. I agreed with him it was best.

When I was finished for the day, he offered to drive me back to the home. It was kind of him, and quite unexpected and would save me a lot of time hanging about for the two buses I normally caught after work. So I gratefully accepted the lift. A short time later, Mr Cameron pulled into the driveway and stopped his car outside the front door of the home. Then he handed me £3.10s. and smiled.

"I can't take your money," I said, pushing his hand away.

"Why?" he asked, looking slightly perplexed.

"I'm not allowed to take money."

"It's your wages."

It was my turn to look puzzled. I wasn't sure what he meant.

"This is the money you've worked for, all week."

"But I'll get into trouble. You keep it."

"Patsy," he explained, slowly. "This is the money you worked all week for. Don't you understand? When you work, you get paid. This is the money, the wages I owe you for that work." Mr Cameron looked at me with an odd expression while shaking his head slowly from side to side. It was as if he couldn't quite believe what he was hearing. He gently offered me the money again, insisting it was mine, and I reluctantly took it. As I made my way into the home, I was worried how I was going to explain having this money and what trouble I would be in for taking it.

The house mother was in the kitchen organising the tea. She looked angry and annoyed and not in the best of moods. I don't think she noticed I was back home. The staff were helping out and getting a bit of a hard time.

"Come on, come on," the house mother snapped at them. "Get a move on." She couldn't stand any slapdash or slovenly ways. No one was as efficient as she was. Everyone else was always far too slow. She darted about here and there and everywhere, barking out orders and checking and double checking the staff had done everything properly. Finally, I managed to catch her attention.

"Yes. What is it?" she replied, not stopping to look at me as she blasted the staff once more, this time for not putting enough tea leaves into the enormous teapot.

"I was given money from Mr Cameron," I said. "I told him to keep it but he said I had to take it as it was the money I worked for."

"Well, why tell me?"

This was not what I expected to hear. Her answer took me by surprise. She wasn't shouting at me for taking the money. I pushed the money towards her.

"What do you expect me to do with it?" she asked. Then, after a pause, she added, "You keep it."

The house mother turned away and carried on with the tea. I walked through to the dining room hardly believing what I'd just heard. Did she really tell me to keep the money? I felt delighted but confused at the same time and more than a little worried she would change her mind at some point. So I decided not spend a penny, just in case. But she never did.

I felt more settled in the job during my second week which seemed to fly past. All the packing went smoothly, without too many hitches, and was all but finished as moving day finally neared. Mr Cameron drove me home again on the Friday and after handing me my wages, told me what the arrangements were for the move to Arbroath the following day. I was to make my way over to the house by midday and then we'd collect the boys from their grandmother and all drive over to the hotel. For the first time, as he was telling me this, it all began to sink in. I really was moving away from Aberdeen, starting afresh, where no one knew me or knew anything about my family.

It was hard to sleep that night knowing it was my last night at the home where I grew up for so many years, protected, naive, smothered, barely noticing the world as it passed me by. Earlier, I went outside on my own, walking around the empty playground for one final time, wondering if anyone would remember me or care that I was ever here. I was filled by an overwhelming desire to do something to mark this moment. Wandering over to the garages and the high wall that hemmed me in for so long, I picked up a stone. While holding it gently in my hand, feeling its smoothness, its timelesness, I said to myself, I will remember you. Then I picked a spot at the bottom of the high wall and carefully buried it.

It was a strange thing to do. It was my goodbye to all the children I knew, to all the laughter we shared, the good times and the sad times, to those who had come and gone. And, like theirs, there was nothing official to mark my passing. But by touching the stone I was now a part of it, connected with it. The stone was part of me. No matter what lay ahead of me in the future, some part of me would still be here, remembered, not forgotten. Often, I wondered if the stone was still there and if it remembered me.

I must have tossed and turned in my bed for hours, playing out all kinds of scenarios in my mind, seeing myself as a nanny and making lots of new friends in strange, exciting surroundings. Thoughts and scenes followed one after the other until tiredness eventually overtook me. When I woke up, the sadness and melancholy of the night before was gone. I felt recharged, positive, looking forward to the start of a new adventure.

No one said anything at the breakfast table, which was unusually quiet. All the children knew I was leaving them soon and I could see in their faces how sad they all felt. But they couldn't tell me. They didn't know how. So their heads remained bowed, fearing any eye contact, concentrating on the bowls of lumpy porridge in front of them. I was glad to leave the table and go to my room. On the way there I told Jennifer I needed something to put my clothes in. So she went to the second-hand cupboard to find me a suitcase.

In my room, I took the few belongings I possessed out of the chest of drawers, neatly folded them and placed them on my bed. The children were now outside playing, so the home was quiet except for the familiar sound of plates being washed and then stacked back in the kitchen cupboards.

Jennifer walked in and handed me a small battered brown suit-case, but not having very much in the way of clothing, it was all I needed. She looked sad helping me pack. I saw she was wishing it was her leaving instead of me, but that could never be. Jennifer was trapped by circumstances, with nowhere to go and no family to turn to. She had no choice in accepting the job as staff, and in my mind I hoped things would get better between her and the house mother. I hoped one day she would find the courage to stand up for herself or find a way to leave.

When the packing was finished and the lid of the suitcase firmly pressed down and fastened, Jennifer told me she would miss me. I felt the tears well up as I told her I would miss her, too. Together, we made our way down the stairs where I said a final goodbye. After buttoning up my jacket, I walked through the empty kitchen and out the back door, heading for the front gate.

As I looked back towards the home for the very last time, I saw the house mother standing by her car which was parked in the driveway. She was deep in conversation with a member of her family. Although she noticed me, her head quickly turned away as I walked the few remaining steps out of the home to the bus stop. There were no wishes of good luck from her, nor even a single goodbye. But I wasn't expecting any. Minutes later, I was gazing out the window of the bus as the busy streets slipped by. They were packed full of Saturday shoppers. I felt scared as I realised I was truly on my own.

When I arrived at the Camerons' home, Mr Cameron was loading a large suitcase into the boot of his car and Mrs Cameron was just stepping out the front door carrying a small blue vanity case. After handing it over to her husband to place in the boot with the rest of the luggage, she turned to greet me.

"Are we all set?" she said, obviously happy to be moving at last.

"Yes," I replied, handing over my suitcase to Mr Cameron who somehow managed to squeeze it in between the rest of the cases and bags.

A short time later we all got in and were on our way to collect the boys. Their grandmother's house turned out to be only a short distance away. As the car entered the long driveway, I was amazed at how big the house was. I was expecting some little bungalow, not the mansion that dwarfed the car. The building was old and beautiful and solid with purple flowers climbing up the front wall. The driveway was awash with colour from different varieties of flowering plants and shrubs growing either side, all adding to the richness of the large and well maintained lawn nearby.

As I looked out the car, I noticed a small boy's face at a downstairs window, peering out from behind white net curtains, waving like mad and smiling as his mother made her way to the front door. Not long afterwards two young boys charged out, heading towards us, and after opening the door dived into the back seat alongside me. The oldest boy was about eight years old and didn't seem to have a bottom to sit on. He fidgeted and bounced on the seat and talked constantly, hardly pausing to take a breath.

"My name is Thomas," he said. "I have leukaemia."

I didn't know at the time what leukaemia was and neither did Thomas, judging by the matter of fact way he said it. Mrs Cameron forgot to mention at the interview he was seriously ill.

"Are you the nanny?" he added in a rather posh, upper crust sort of voice.

Without giving me a chance to reply, he said, "This is Morgan. He's five!"

Thomas hogged the conversation, never allowing his brother a moment to speak for himself. I only managed to slip in the odd word or two, nothing more, until his father told him sternly to settle down and wave to his grandmother now standing outside the front door. It was obvious the children were very happy to be reunited once more with their parents and excited about moving to their new home.

But was I taking on more than I could handle? It was going to be a hard job looking after them. As we pulled out the driveway and into the main road, baby James was fast asleep in his mother's arms, the only one unaware of the new adventure ahead.

Chapter Fourteen

IT TOOK US LESS than an hour to reach the hotel which was situated in the middle of the town. Mr Cameron took me up to my room and told me to take the weekend to settle in and get used to the place before starting work on the Monday. It felt odd having a room of my own. The peace and quiet was a bit unnerving. But I quickly began to enjoy the feeling of privacy.

The room was fairly big with a single window. It was simply furnished with two double beds and a chest of drawers for my clothes. But with the two beds, there was not a great deal of space left to move around. The room was built into the roof so was at the very top of the hotel. It formed part of the private quarters used by Mr and Mrs Cameron and the children.

Directly underneath lay some dozen rooms for the guests. The rooms were evenly split between the first and second floors. A wide staircase led down from the room corridors to a large dining area and a bar on the ground floor. The hotel, with a history going back more than 200 years, was decorated with flowery wallpaper. Deep luxurious red carpeting covered the floor throughout. Small tables with pot plants and ornaments on top filled the hotel's many little nooks and crannies. Subdued lighting added to the homely comfortable atmosphere. I loved the place.

As I emptied out my suitcase and placed the few clothes I possessed into the chest of drawers, I was distinctly aware of being watched by an old man. The impression was strong and powerful and unmistakable. But when I turned around, there was nobody there. Although I felt slightly uneasy, I wasn't at all frightened by the strange feeling. I experienced the same thing many times over in the weeks and months ahead. Towards the end of my stay at the hotel I shared the room with a waitress who hated being in there on her own. When I asked her why, she said the room creeped her out. It felt as if there was always someone else in the room. I told her I had the same feeling, which made her a lot happier because she thought she was going mad. It confirmed that what I was experiencing was real and not a figment of my imagination. But beyond that, I didn't question or think too deeply about it all. The presence was there and not out to harm me. So I just accepted it.

☙❧

I was alone in the upstairs quarters, finding the silence difficult to come to terms with. There were no guests in the hotel yet and the Camerons were all out for the afternoon, shopping for school uniforms for the boys. I was bored, too, so I decided to explore the streets and shops outside. Passing by a tobacconists', a cigarette advertisement in the shop window caught my eye.

When I was young I often imagined myself as the famous Hollywood actress Bette Davis. I slinked about the home acting all grown up and sophisticated, blowing imaginary smoke from the pencil held between my two fingers. Now I was old enough to buy a packet of cigarettes for real, and there was nobody to tell me I couldn't. There was also money in my purse. So I bought a packet of 10 menthol cigarettes and walked over to a nearby park and sat on a bench. I was determined to savour this moment.

Unwinding the cellophane wrapper and opening the packet, I
pulled off the silver paper covering the top of the cigarettes and
crumpled it into a small ball. Casually, I tossed it away. Taking a
cigarette out slowly, enjoying the firm feel and texture of the
paper surrounding the tobacco, I gently placed it in between my
two fingers. This was the real thing, not some childish pencil. I felt
grown up, an adult, the mistress of my own destiny. Bringing the
cigarette up to my mouth and placing it in between my lips, I
struck a match and lit up, drawing in a long, deep breath.

Suddenly, the world coughed and spluttered to a grinding halt.
I struggled for breath. My whole body heaved and shook in uncon-
trollable fits. The park spun round and round. I felt sick to my toes.
Naive childhood fantasies lay shattered. I threw the packet on the
ground and angrily stamped it into the dirt until it turned into an
unrecognisable mess. When the bitter acrid taste swirling about in
my mouth finally subsided a little, I made my way back to the
hotel vowing never to smoke another cigarette in my life.

Monday came quickly and because I didn't have an alarm clock I
was wakened up by Mrs Cameron. While she looked after the baby,
I helped the boys get ready for school and then spent the next
hour sorting out their clothes and tidying up. When Mrs Cameron
disappeared downstairs, to work in the hotel, I took over looking
after baby James. He was around eight months old, sturdy with
blond curly hair, blue eyes and a cheeky loveable smile. James was
a happy baby and hardly ever cried. I fed him and changed him and
then took him out for a walk in his pram. When the boys came
home from school, I also looked after their needs, so evenings
were always very busy for me until their bedtimes. Only then did I
have a few moments to myself.

Weekdays were easy by comparison to the weekends. The hotel was particularly busy on a Saturday and the Camerons were tied up downstairs all day and late into the evening, so I never saw them. All the responsibility of looking after the children fell squarely on my shoulders. It was a huge responsibility for someone just turned 15.

Sometimes the older boys played together nicely. But most times, they were at each other's throats, arguing and shouting and I found myself in the middle trying to sort things out while still having to watch the baby. At the end of the day I felt exhausted. I was always thankful when Sunday dawned. It was my only day off in the week, the only time I felt I could relax a little.

About a month into the job, Thomas became very ill because of his leukaemia and was rushed into the hospital in Aberdeen. Later on that day, I noticed Mrs Cameron sitting in Thomas's room on his bed looking very down. The bedroom door was wide open. As I entered the room, she looked up at me and we started talking.

She told me that giving birth to Thomas nearly killed her when she lived in South Africa. There was resentment in her voice which I couldn't help but notice. It made me wonder if that was the reason why she never seemed to give him much affection or have very much time for him. I was certainly taken aback by what she said. It made me feel awkward. I didn't know what to say to her. So I made an excuse and left to go downstairs.

When I walked into the dining room, I was surprised to see an old lady standing there. On the floor beside her was a small suitcase. She looked unusual to say the least, dressed in a plastic flowery raincoat and a matching plastic hat. The flowery pattern was repeated on her plastic wellington boots. I didn't know what to make of her. The heavy white powder covering her face made her look deathly pale and accentuated the bright red ruby lipstick plastering her lips.

"And who might you be?" she demanded, in a rather loud aristocratic English-sounding voice.

"I'm the nanny," I replied, rather meekly.

"Well, I'm the children's grandmother. I want you to go upstairs and tell my daughter I've arrived. Tell her to come downstairs. I want to see her."

With a flick of her hand, she shooed me away. She was a rather bossy old lady whose fingers were covered in gold and diamond rings. Even I could see she was used to getting her own way. I met her again later on as we all sat down in the dining room for the evening meal. She told her family she was flying from Aberdeen to London to do some shopping in Carnaby Street and then planned to take in a West End show. So she was only staying the one night. As I looked at her across the table, I thought to myself her dress style was so over the top for an old lady. The chitchat was all about holidays and parties and society and only underlined the wealth and circles they all belonged to and moved in. I already knew the family was extremely rich and that I was working for millionaires. Now, for the first time, I began to see the sort of lifestyle they all enjoyed and took for granted.

The evening meal was a struggle for me. I felt so out of place, coming from such a humble background and having nothing in common with them. So most of the time I sat quietly, hardly touching my food, never taking part in the conversation.

As the days and weeks passed, my sense of isolation and unhappiness only grew. I felt desperately lonely and realised I was missing the kids from the home. Eventually, Mrs Cameron noticed how much weight I was losing and how uncomfortable I always appeared sitting at the table. So she asked me if I would be happier eating my meals with the staff in the kitchen. I said I would.

∽

One day, out of the blue, a young waitress at the hotel started to chat away to me. She hadn't been in the job very long and like me, was struggling to know what was expected of her. She told me her name was Elizabeth and this was her first job since leaving school.

Elizabeth asked me if I wanted to go to the dancing with her and her friends and I jumped at the chance. So we arranged to go on my day off and agreed to meet outside the front entrance of the hotel. The dance was held in what looked like an old community hall. As we entered, there was deafening music and flashing coloured disco lights. The small dance floor was so packed with teenagers there was hardly any room to move. The music and the atmosphere and the sheer joy and fun of the occasion went straight to my head. Before I knew it, I was dancing and jumping about all over the place. One after the other, boys came up to me and started dancing and the evening flew by in a flash.

Suddenly, I was brought back down to earth by a sharp kick up the backside. I spun around furiously to see a girl wearing a smirky grin. Then she laughed at me and I wanted to punch her face in. Before I had the chance to Elizabeth intervened, dragging me away, calming me down. It was nearly ten, she reminded me. Time to go. Mrs Cameron warned us to be back at the hotel by then. So we left the dancing.

As we walked back, I kept thinking about the incident, trying to understand why the girl kicked me for no reason. Although I couldn't figure it out, I felt more disturbed by my own reaction. This was the first time I realised what a temper I had. But it was all forgotten about by the time we reached the hotel.

When I climbed the stairs and entered the private quarters, I noticed the baby's room was open, so I went in to check on him. The room was fairly dark with only the hall light shining through. But I could clearly see baby James sitting on the floor with his back to me, playing with his toys.

Surprised, I turned to look at his cot, wondering how on earth he could have got out of it. But he was also in there, lying fast asleep. I looked back again and there he was, still sitting on the floor, happily playing on the carpet. I couldn't understand what I was seeing.

Almost in a panic, I dashed through to Mrs Cameron's room and told her James was on the carpet. Then I followed her as she ran through to his room where she made straight for the cot.

"What are you talking about?" she said, sounding rather annoyed but with relief showing in her face. "He's fast asleep."

She was right. James was no longer on the carpet but in his cot and as I tried to explain what I saw she looked at me as if I was some kind of nutcase. She told me to stop talking nonsense and suggested I go to my bed. Later, as I puzzled over what I saw, I felt more than a little foolish.

Mrs Cameron never really mentioned the incident again except for one cryptic passing comment, a couple of days later, when she talked about meeting strange people like me when she lived in South Africa. I didn't have a clue what she was talking about and she never explained any further.

Sometimes, on my days off, I went through and played on the old piano in the corner of the empty morning room. The morning room formed part of the private quarters. The Camerons planned to convert it into a sitting room for the family. But all it contained at that time was the piano and a stool to sit on.

I was becoming increasingly unhappy in my job. Mrs Cameron only made matters worse by having less and less to do with the children. This increased the pressure and demands placed on me. She even became convinced I was pregnant, although I told her repeatedly I wasn't. But she never believed me and insisted I provide a sample of urine for the doctor to check. Somehow, I think she got the idea because I started going out on a couple of dates with a boy I met at the dancing. He was a good-looking boy with platinum blond hair. But there was nothing in the relationship. We were both just 15. He ditched his girlfriend just before asking me out for the first time. She was was the girl who kicked me up the backside. No doubt she was jealous because he was one of the boys up dancing with me that night. When he walked me back, he always gave me a good-night kiss in front of the hotel. More to keep Mrs Cameron off my back, I gave in and provided the urine sample.

One day I was alone in the morning room when I was startled by two men wearing long dark coats and trilby hats suddenly walking in.

"Are you Patricia Whyte?" the older of the two demanded.

"Yes," I stammered nervously.

"We're police detectives. We'd like you to come with us to the station."

"Why? What's happened? What's wrong?"

There was neither an answer nor any explanation or any smiles of reasurance. They looked serious and intimidating, all the time insisting I put my coat on and go with them. My throat was dry and my legs trembled. I grabbed my coat and walked in between them, down the main staircase of the hotel, watched from a distance by the staff who all stopped working. Mr and Mrs Cameron were nowhere to be seen.

A few seconds later I was outside and heading towards a waiting car, feeling bewildered, my stomach in knots. One of the detectives opened the back door and pushed me inside and we drove away. The journey to the police station only lasted a few minutes. I was ushered out of the car and led past a uniformed constable at the front desk to a sparsely furnished side room. There was a table in the centre of the room on which lay a large black ink-pad. A single chair stood up against one of the whitewashed walls.

Before I knew it, one of the detectives pulled up the sleeves of my coat and without permission pressed my fingers and thumbs into the ink-pad. Then he rolled each one onto a piece of white card. He told me to stand next to the wall and not to smile. A flash of bright light blinded me for a second or two. I was ordered to sit down on the chair. Only then did they tell me what it was all about. Someone broke into the hotel's electric meter and stole the money inside. Did I do it?

"No," was my one and only word of reply.

I couldn't think straight as they bombarded me with question after question, asking me what I was doing and where I was on Friday night. The interrogation continued for about ten minutes, but it seemed to last much longer than that. Suddenly, the questions stopped. They glanced at each other. Then one of them told me they were taking me back to the hotel. Within a couple of minutes I was standing outside the hotel entrance watching the car and the detectives driving off and disappearing out of sight. Still feeling shaky and upset, I drew a deep breath and walked inside. The first person I saw was Elizabeth. She appeared concerned and asked me what happened.

"The police are saying I broke into the hotel meters and stole money. I don't even know what a meter is or what it looks like," I said.

"That's terrible," gasped Elizabeth.

"Did they ask you questions?"

"No, they never," she said.

"What about any of the rest of the staff?"

"No. No one," she replied.

I didn't know what to make of it all. Other members of staff who saw me come in were now watching us. Whenever they noticed me looking back at them, heads turned away or stared at the floor. They couldn't look me in the eye. It was then I knew I was guilty as far as they were concerned, a thief, accused and convicted without a shred of evidence against me. The atmosphere felt so bad I couldn't stand it any longer and I headed upstairs to my room.

On the way there, I bumped into Mrs Cameron. By the reaction on her face, I was the last person she expected to see. I realised then she must have blamed me for the break-in and called the police. From that moment onwards, I knew I had to leave the hotel. How could I continue to work for someone who thought so little of me, who was now making me out to be a thief? My position here was impossible. There was nothing else left for me to do.

Over the next few days, I made the best of a bad situation, avoiding talking to Mrs Cameron as much as I could. All the time, she acted as if nothing happened, which I found very odd. But the damage was done as far as I was concerned. It was only a matter of picking the right moment to tell her I was leaving. Until then, I needed time to think. I didn't know what to do or how to go about leaving and finding somewhere else to stay. There was no one to turn to for advice.

My mind was still in a quandary on my day off. As it was such a beautiful morning, I decided to grab a breath of fresh air to escape the hotel for a few hours. Outside in the street, I passed the public entrance to the hotel bar and glanced through the open door. Something made me stop dead in my tracks.

A man was sitting drinking a pint. When I looked at him I knew instantly he was the thief. I couldn't explain it but it was an all-knowing feeling. As I stared at him, he stared back at me and it made him feel so uncomfortable he turned his head away. He was smartly dressed and in his early thirties with curly brown hair. I was certain that he knew I knew what he had done. But what could I do? Who would believe me? Certainly not Mr Cameron serving behind the bar.

Later on that evening, there was some good news and some bad news. Mrs Cameron told me I wasn't pregnant after all. The urine sample came back negative from the doctor, just as I knew it would. But I was apparently going to die.

"You're seriously ill," she said. "Don't you understand?"

I saw she was getting a little upset at my indifferent attitude. If she was expecting me to break down or to take her seriously then she was very much mistaken. I didn't care any more and I didn't even bother answering her as I walked to my room.

There was a buzz in the air when I came downstairs the next day and walked into the dining room. Elizabeth rushed over to me and told me the thief had been caught. As soon as she described him, I knew it was the same man I saw sitting in the public bar. The attitude of the rest of the members of staff now changed towards me, becoming warm and friendly instead of distant and cold. But there was never a hint of an apology from Mr and Mrs Cameron.

I felt now was the time to tell Mrs Cameron I was leaving. I waited until she was alone and then announced the news. She was shocked and tried to bribe me to stay, offering to buy me new dresses and to take me to South Africa on holiday with the family. I refused and despite further attempts to make me change my mind, she finally accepted I was going to leave. So she suggested I fill in as a waitress at the hotel until something was organised.

In the meantime, I decided to telephone the house mother at the home to ask for advice. I didn't know who else to turn to. As I dialled the number, I felt resentful inside at having to ask her for help. But there was an anger growing inside me and a determination to get as far away as I could from the Camerons.

"I'm not staying here," I told the house mother, after explaining it all. "I just want to leave, but I've nowhere to go."

The telephone went silent. There followed a long pause, but I was hopeful the house mother would understand the predicament I was in. But there were no words of comfort from her. Instead she passed me on to Allan. I thought to myself, how could he know? He only left the home a year before me. So what was he doing there?

Allan's voice was calm and reassuring. The boy who grew up with me all those years was now this mature voice on the telephone, telling me not to worry. He was going to contact the social workers and see if they could send someone out to the hotel to see me. I said thanks and put the receiver down.

Feeling much happier than for a very long time, there was a bit of skip in my step as I went back to my room. When I turned the handle, the door wouldn't open. I was locked out. So I found Mrs Cameron and asked her for a spare key. But there was no spare key. Mr Cameron volunteered to climb out onto the roof through the window of the room next door. Mrs Cameron was horrified at the thought because the roof was more than 40 feet above the ground. But she couldn't stop him. The colour drained from her face.

"Richard, Richard," she howled. "Remember what your astrological chart predicted. Please come back in."

But he ignored her plea and gingerly inched the few feet across the roof to my window. Fortunately, it was open. He slid through into my room without too much difficulty and let me back in. Exactly what the dire astrological prediction was I never knew. The prediction must have been wrong. It certainly got Mrs Cameron in a fluster.

The days which followed crawled by at a snail's pace. I was only going through the motions of being a waitress, nothing more. Keeping busy helped me to concentrate on something other than my present difficulties. Although Mrs Cameron made a huge effort to be nice and friendly towards me, I still didn't feel comfortable around her. She tried to play the part of the concerned employer, asking me if I liked the job and how I felt I was coping. But it was all pretence. I saw right through it all.

The dining room was quiet. Earlier, it was very busy and I was rushed off my feet with hardly a moment to myself. The tables were cleared and now awaited the arrival of any hotel guests who wanted to take high tea later on in the afternoon. The temporary lull also allowed me the time to pop into the kitchen to grab some leftovers. I poured myself a lemonade and put two scoops of icecream in the glass. This was my favourite drink, which I liked far too much. I understood now why Mrs Cameron thought I was pregnant. Since taking meals in the kitchen, where I almost had a free hand, my weight ballooned from all the rich food available.

The break lasted half an hour and then it was back to work again. I heard the dining room door click open as guests started to wander through and sit down for tea. I was on my own. Gone were the other two waitresses who normally worked alongside me over the dinner period. They were at home and no doubt glad of the half-day off to rest throbbing feet.

Mrs Cameron was already on duty in the dining room. As I passed her, my eyes nearly popped out of their sockets. Sitting at a table no more than four or five feet from me was the house mother and some of her relatives. I wanted to about-turn and run back into the safety of the kitchen. But I knew I couldn't. I just stood rooted to the spot, staring in disbelief. Mrs Cameron broke the silence. "Patricia, would you like to serve them tea?"

Mrs Cameron addressed them all by name and seemed much too friendly, so I assumed they'd already met earlier for a chat. After a quick nod of the head, I hastily made my way back to the kitchen, hating the idea of having to serve the house mother and pretend all the years at the home were now forgotten. Maybe she could forget how badly she treated me but I was still raw inside.

The house mother neither acknowledged my existence nor uttered a single word to me as I served her. Her relatives were all just as silent as she was. Mrs Cameron tried to break the ice, suggesting I sit at the table for a little while. Although I nodded in agreement, I made an excuse to get back into the kitchen to avoid the very uncomfortable situation. I was glad when more guests walked in. Serving them meant I didn't have to talk to the house mother. When I turned to look at her table a short time later, she was gone.

The hotel staff were a lot more friendly towards me than before, trying hard in their own way to make up for wrongly thinking me a thief. I suppose they felt guilty, wanting to put the whole episode behind them, which I was more than happy to do. Even the cook, a lady in her thirties, allowed me to help myself to any food in the kitchen whenever I was hungry. One of the older waitresses started to confide in me, telling me all the problems she had living with her husband. He drank their money away at the pub. Whenever she confronted him, they had furious rows. He promised to change but she wasn't convinced. She was unsure whether to leave him or to stay and work it all out.

Several days later, I was in the kitchen at the end of a busy lunch time, piling cups and saucers onto a tray ready to lay the tables for afternoon tea. Mrs Cameron suddenly appeared and told me to stop what I was doing and follow her through to the dining room.

Standing near one of the empty tables was a young woman. She was in her early twenties, smart but casually dressed, with long dark hair falling across her shoulders. After introducing herself as my social worker, she told me to get my belongings together. I was leaving. She had managed to find me somewhere else to stay. Hardly able to hide my delight, I ran upstairs to my room to pack. It took me no more than a couple of minutes to pile the few clothes I had into my battered brown suitcase and head downstairs again. I wasn't at all sorry to be leaving. But I was surprised how quickly events had suddenly moved. Perhaps it was something to do with the visit by the house mother. I never understood why she turned up out of the blue and then disappeared just as quickly.

Whatever the reason, my one and only regret was having to leave the hotel staff. I was really getting to know them well. They completely accepted me. Elizabeth was a good friend now and I was sorry not to be able to say goodbye. That was really hard. The social worker asked me if I was all set to go and I said I was. As I sat in the back seat of her small car, being driven through the streets and then out into the countryside, I still didn't know where I was going.

"Where am I going to live?" I asked, starting to worry about the social worker's complete silence on the subject.

"I've managed to get you some accommodation at a girls' hostel," she said eventually.

"I'm not living there," I replied instantly.

Visions of living in a place similar to the home I lived in all my life filled me with dread. I had only just escaped and now I was being thrown back in. The social worker sensed the worry and anguish in my voice.

"It's only temporary," she reassured me. "It's only for two weeks until I find something more suitable for you."

There was nothing I could do. Arbroath was far behind me now. Although upset and a little bit wary, I reasoned that two weeks wasn't very long and I could survive that. The time would soon pass and then I'd be somewhere better. It wasn't very fair to put so much pressure on my new social worker who was only trying to do her best by me.

The car drove through the now familiar busy streets of Aberdeen. I felt a sense of calm after deciding to look upon it all as yet another adventure, another new phase in my life. If only I knew then what lay ahead of me, I would surely have ran away as far as I could at the first opportunity.

Chapter Fifteen

THE CAR PULLED UP OUTSIDE the large grey granite house. It was an imposing building, solid, surrounded by monkey puzzle trees that hid it from the outside world. There were no flowers or bushes anywhere to brighten up its dullness. I stood next to my social worker in front of the heavy wood-panelled front door. Nervously, she straightened out her skirt and brushed a few imaginary creases away with her fingers before ringing the doorbell.

A moment or two later, a lady dressed in white overalls stood in front of us. She was huge, the spare tyre around her middle placing an almost impossible strain on buttons threatening to fly off in all directions at any moment. A dusting of white flour covered her dark hair which was tied up into a tight pony tail, giving her the appearance of someone who was much older. My social worker explained who we were.

"Yes, the house mother's expecting you. If you'd like to come this way," said the lady. There was no trace of emotion anywhere in her voice. She quickly led us along a wide hallway to a green coloured door and stopped outside it. After two quick raps with her knuckles, she turned the large solid brass door handle and ushered us through.

The house mother sat behind a desk in the middle of the room, head buried in some kind of report. Her eyes barely looked up as we entered. She reminded me of the stern prison wardens I'd seen in films. Large black heavy-framed glasses sat perched halfway down her nose. Her hair was tightly drawn off her face into a bun at the back of her head.

As I looked around the room, which doubled as both office and sitting room, I felt the chill from her cold demeanour and I started to cry. I knew no warmth was to be found in my new home. She glanced up from the report she was so engrossed in and her eyes met mine.

"You can stop that right now. Those tears won't wash here!" she snapped.

Her words cut straight through me and made me grip the handle of my suitcase even tighter. My social worker said nothing in my defence and quickly excused herself. All of a sudden, she was late for another appointment. Before I knew it she was gone and I was on my own, listening to the sound of her footsteps walking down the corridor and fading in the distance.

The house mother said nothing. She motioned me to follow her out of the room. We stopped in the dining area. There I noticed the same type of blue plastic plates used in the home. They were all laid out on the large table in the centre, ready for the evening meal. She broke the silence, laying down the law with a list of rules.

"This is where you will come to eat," she said. "If you are late, you won't get a meal. You are allowed to go out two evenings a week until 9 o'clock. Any later and the police will be called. You hand all of your wages over to me on a Friday, straight after work. You do not open your wage packet. You bring it straight into my living room and then hand it over. Do you understand?"

"Yes," I replied meekly, feeling more miserable with each passing second.

"And," staring directly at me as if to measure each word carefully for effect, she slowly added, "you do exactly as you are told to do. When I ask you to do something, you jump to it. Do I make myself clear?"

There was no need for me to reply. It wasn't expected. The fear written all over my face was enough. She knew I got the message loud and clear. After pointing me in the direction of my room, the house mother turned her back on me and walked away. I don't think I had ever felt so alone in the world as I did at that moment. The only thing keeping me going was the promise my social worker made. I was only here for two weeks, just while she found another place for me, and I couldn't wait.

I climbed the main staircase to my room which I found easily enough and planted my suitcase down on the floor. The room was bright and airy and held three single beds and three chests of drawers. Green flowery wallpaper covered the walls and matched in with the bedspreads. Knick-knacks and other personal items lay neatly on top of two of the chests of drawers. I assumed rightly the one with nothing on top was mine, so I picked up my suitcase and placed it on the bed next to it and unpacked.

During the evening meal I finally met up with my room-mates and the rest of the girls at the hostel. The hostel was empty and quiet up until then. I stayed hidden in my room out of sight of the house mother, not wanting to cross paths with her if I could help it. But now I couldn't avoid her. She was sitting at the dining table. The house mother said nothing. She never so much as looked at me as I took my place at the table. Neither did any of the other eight or nine girls. They must have noticed me yet they didn't talk to me or even acknowledge I was there.

The dining room was fairly large with a carpeted floor. It was dominated by the highly polished table we were sitting at. Food brought through from the kitchen was ready and waiting in the warming drawers of a large trolley pushed up against the far wall. When the house mother nodded, one of the girls got up and served the food.

I found sitting amongst complete strangers a real strain. Throughout the meal, I never uttered a single word, apart from a quiet but polite thank you when food was served onto my plate. So I watched and listened to them all. Quickly, I realised the conversation was more about scoring Brownie points. The girls wanted to please the house mother all the time. They were very careful not to say or do anything which she might find fault with. It was obvious she enjoyed the power she held over them. The whole performance reminded me of a game of cat and mouse. Ruby, one of the girls, talked excitedly about the boy she just got engaged to whom she'd been going out with for some time. She tried her best to appear casual, waving and moving her hand a lot through the air so we would take note of the new engagement ring on her finger. Her friends seemed impressed. I wasn't. Neither was the house mother.

Dinner was over quite quickly because most of the girls were in a hurry to get ready to go out for the evening. I hung about the sitting room and watched television. An older girl with long brown waist-length hair, dressed in a brightly coloured top and long skirt, walked in and started raking about looking for something. She was small and weasily and her thin frame lay hidden underneath her loose flowing clothes. She reminded me of a hippie. When she didn't find what she was looking for, she started pulling cushions off the chairs and flinging them to the floor. Without saying a word, she moved over to the settee where a pile of magazines lay neatly stacked. The magazines also ended up tossed and scattered across the room.

"There's a thief in here," she finally bellowed out, so I would hear.

I ignored her and carried on watching television until she deliberately stood in front of me.

"Did you take my cigarettes?" she demanded, in an American accent. "Are you a bloody thief?"

"Who are you calling a thief? I never touched them!" I screamed back. I felt irritated by her antics and attitude. The stress of the move and living in a strange place was difficult enough to come to terms with, so I wasn't in the mood for any of this crap.

"Maybe you put them down somewhere else," I shouted. "Try looking before you start blaming me."

"Huh. We'll see."

We glared at each other for a moment. Then she threw her head in the air and stormed out of the sitting room, leaving me with the feeling we'd be anything but best friends. I decided to go to bed early because I was exhausted and felt down and wanted to be left on my own. There was no way I was looking for any further confrontation, either with her or with anyone else.

My head no sooner hit the pillow than I was fast asleep. But not long afterwards, I was wakened up by my room-mates returning from their evening out. They seemed bubbly and happy and asked me all kinds of questions. One of the girls was aged about 17 and was called Jen. She was small with black hair feathered in at the back and worked as an usherette at a cinema. She had spent the evening at her boyfriend's house listening to Jimi Hendrix records and loved "Purple Haze". Joy, my other room-mate, was a little taller than Jen with short blonde wavy hair. She wasn't as fashionably dressed and worked behind the counter in Boots the Chemist. I got the feeling she was the sort of person who would be there for life. Her poor boyfriend took second place next to her job.

Before we all went to sleep, Jen warned me to watch out for the house mother. She was a bitch. The girl with the American accent

was Kirsty, a single parent. She was right in with the house mother
and liked to grass people up.

Next day, I found out the fat lady in the white overalls was the
cook. She seemed to have a lot of say in the running of the hostel
and the welfare of the girls. The cook told me to stop moping
about all day and get myself down to the employment exchange
and find a job. So I did and got myself a job in a biscuit factory. It
was a good job. All I had to do was carry trays of biscuits from the
processing machines and stack them onto huge racks. I was
allowed to eat as many biscuits as I wanted. It was great at first,
until I sickened myself. On Friday, after work, I handed my wages
over to the house mother as instructed. Jen told me she was
supposed to hand me back ten shillings. But this never happened.
So it meant I had no make-up or clothes to go out with. Maybe I
should have said something. But I didn't because I knew I would
have to practically beg for it. I wasn't prepared to do that.

Day after day, I kept looking out the window for the white car
belonging to my social worker. But she never came and my heart
sank deeper into despair. I finally plucked up the courage to ask
the house mother when she was coming back.

"What nonsense are you talking about? There's no one coming,"
she said, obviously enjoying my disappointment.

At that moment I realised I'd been betrayed, abandoned,
dumped, left here to rot. I'd been well and truly conned and I felt
the anger rising inside me as I turned to walk away. I thought to
myself, I'm not going to be controlled any more. I'm out of here
the first chance I get and no one's going to stop me.

When I awoke next morning, feeling tired and drained after
tossing and turning all night, I was late for work. I leapt out of bed
quickly throwing my clothes on and dashed out the door to catch
the bus. The bus was full so I climbed up the stairs and grabbed the
first empty seat I saw. Then pulling at the hem of my mini skirt, to

make sure I was decent, I slid across the seat to the window. Something didn't feel right. The seat felt unusually cold. Oh my God! I thought to myself. I'm not wearing any knickers. In my rush to get ready, I forgot to put them on. I carefully made my way downstairs and got off at the next stop and walked back to the hostel feeling rather foolish. Thankfully, no one spotted me as I darted into my room and then out again to catch the bus once more to work. When I finally arrived, I was called through to the manager's office to explain why I was late. Terrified, I stood in front of him and explained my predicament. Instead of firing me, as I expected, he burst out laughing. My face was red with embarrassment but at least my job was safe.

When I collected my wages on Friday, I decided to open the packet and take ten shillings out before handing it over to the house mother. She was not going to take all of my wages this time and leave me with nothing. I worked hard all week for the money. After carefully sealing the packet up again, I went into her office and handed it over. My fingers were crossed hoping she wouldn't notice the money was missing, but my luck was out. Within minutes, she marched through to the sitting room with a face like thunder and ordered me to follow her.

"Explain yourself!" she demanded angrily, thumping her fist on to the desk where my opened wage packet lay. "Where is the rest of the money?"

"I took the money out," I said, defiantly.

"Hand it over now," she shouted.

"I don't have it."

She knew I was lying and her face grew even more red with anger.

"What do you mean you don't have it?"

"I've spent it!"

She paused for a moment with a stunned, shocked expression

on her face. No one ever stood up to her like this before. "What did I tell you the rules were about wages?"

"To hand them unopened to you," I said.

She paused. My hatred of her grew with each passing second. I refused to be intimidated as she tried to stare me down. She was going to be the first to blink, not me. And she did. Maybe for the first time, she realised there was nothing she could do.

"Get out of my sight. Don't think this is the last of it. I'll deal with you later."

I knew I was in for a hard time now but I didn't care any more. The house mother could do what she wanted or give me any punishment but I was going to make life extremely difficult for her, too. True to her word, it started the next day when the cook handed me the biggest pot she could find and told me to start peeling potatoes and fill it.

Bloody hell, I thought to myself. I'll be here till midnight!

All the while, the cook hovered about making sure I didn't slacken for a single moment. Hours later, or so it seemed, the job was finally done. I went through to the television room. Kirsty was there with a couple of the other girls she was friendly with. As soon as I sat down, they began to snigger and whisper amongst themselves. They were talking about me, making sure I heard the odd remark. It wasn't the first time they acted in this way when I was around them, so their annoying behaviour was not entirely unexpected. I could see the girls who hung about with Kirsty were just using her, because she kept them supplied with cigarettes and money she collected from the DHSS to support her and her son. It was all so pathetic.

On the Sunday, I was ordered back into the kitchen where the cook pointed to a large shelf filled with heavy steel pots and pans. She told me to scrub every single one of them until they all gleamed brightly. She disappeared out of the kitchen and I filled the white stone sink with hot soapy water. A minute later, the cook returned pulling a wooden stepladder behind her.

"Use that to climb up to the pots and start scrubbing," she ordered. This was the house mother's revenge. As I set about the task, my mood changed from dark to black and brooding. The more pots I cleaned, the harder I slammed each one down on the draining board. Kirsty wandered through, watching me. Then she began to snigger as I pulled another heavy pot off the shelf. The cook was also enjoying herself, constantly on my back, ordering me to clean the same pot over and over because it was not shiny enough, even though I could practically see my face in it. While I was reaching for one more pot, Kirsty deliberately pushed the stepladder. I nearly fell off. She burst out laughing watching me grab on to the shelf to steady myself, like it was all some kind of game. The pot slipped out of my fingers and tumbled to the floor with a crash.

In an instant, something snapped inside me. I flew down the ladder like lightning and grabbed the cook with both hands, flinging her hard against the wall. Eyes wide open with fear, mouth gaping, eighteen stones of flab slithered down and crumbled into a heap on the floor. I grabbed a large carving knife and bolted after Kirsty who was now howling and screaming at the top of her voice, running up the road for dear life. Possessed, a mad woman, hell-bent on catching her at any cost, I was oblivious to everything going on around me in this normally peaceful street. I must have run at least a quarter of a mile. But I couldn't find her. By then, the rage inside me was beginning to subside. Feeling shaky and shocked, and still holding the knife in my hand, I suddenly felt disgusted with myself. For I had no idea such anger existed inside me and that I was capable of hurting someone. So I threw the knife away into a clump of nearby bushes and slowly walked back to the hostel.

Things didn't get any better for me as I went back into the kitchen to face the cook. She was still more than a little shook up and now extremely wary of me. "I've called your social worker," she said. "She's coming straight up to have words with you. You're in for it now." And, she added, menacingly, "The house mother's coming back. She'll sort you out. She's a black belt in karate."

I took the cook's words as some sort of warning. But I didn't care whether the house mother's belt was pink, black or green. She didn't frighten me any more. Towards the end of the afternoon, when the house mother finally appeared on the scene, there was no great battle or confrontation. Although the cook obviously told her what happened, the house mother decided to let the social worker sort me out. Kirsty, meanwhile, crept quietly back to her room and locked the door.

The rest of the girls returned back in dribs and drabs during the early evening after spending the day out visiting boyfriends or relatives. I'd made good friends with one of them, Sadie, who liked nothing more than to clown around and impersonate the house mother or the cook, which usually had me in stitches. A bit of a tomboy, she was considered a real hard case and everyone was frightened of her except me. We seemed to click right away. Sadie asked me what was wrong when she noticed I wasn't laughing at any of her jokes. I told her of my run-in with the cook and Kirsty.

"I can't stand her big mouth," she said. "That bitch is always sucking up to the house mother. She needs sorting out!"

"Yeah, go on, you sort her out," I said, unsure whether Sadie was actually joking or not.

We were interrupted by the cook. My social worker was here and wanted to speak to me in the office. I expected to see a familiar face as I walked in, not the lady now standing before me. She was someone completely different, smartly dressed, in her late forties with short wavy honey-blonde hair. The silk autumn-coloured scarf tied around her neck perfectly complemented the green suit she was wearing.

She introduced herself as Mrs Strachan and then asked the cook to leave us as she wanted to speak to me in private. But the cook refused, saying she was standing in for the house mother who was tied up with some other business and couldn't be here. This annoyed Mrs Strachan who pointed out the confidential nature of the meeting. But it made no difference. The cook still insisted on staying.

"I'll be reporting this," Mrs Strachan snapped back.

She then asked me how I was doing in my job and was I buying any new clothes?

"No," I said.

"You must have money in your bank book?"

I shrugged my shoulders.

"Do you have a bank book?"

Once more, I simply shrugged my shoulders without saying anything. My new social worker looked hard at the cook. "Can you get me her bank book? I'd like to look at it."

The cook replied, "She doesn't have any money in her bank book."

Mrs Strachan, looking surprised, said, "I can't understand that. She must have money in her bank book. She's working. It can't all go on board. Please get me her bank book."

The cook was having none of it. She still refused to get it. Mrs Strachan was annoyed but had to accept the brick wall she was up against. But she fired a parting shot as she got up to leave.

"I'm going to get this investigated," she warned, staring hard at the cook with fixed steely-blue eyes. "You can tell the house mother I will be back to see Patricia and this time I will see her in private."

With that, she walked smartly out the room leaving the cook in no doubt she meant business. As I made my way back to the sitting room, for the first time I felt I had someone fighting my corner for me. It was a good feeling. I knew I was going to like Mrs Strachan.

While I was in the office, Sadie was banging on Kirsty's door, trying to get her to come out. I knew nothing of this at the time and only caught the tail end of a very one-sided conversation as I climbed the stairs to go to my room. Sadie cursed and swore and turned the air a very deep shade of blue. "You start on my friend again and I'll beat the living daylights out of your smug ugly face," she shouted, as she hammered relentlessly on the door. She calmed right down when she noticed me at the top of the stairs. "That'll teach her. She'll think twice before giving you a hard time again."

A big grin came over her face. I could see she was enjoying it all, acting the hard case, terrorising Kirsty and any of the other girls within earshot. Needless to say, Kirsty took a very long time to emerge from her room. She never bothered me again.

Chapter Sixteen

THE JOB AT THE BISCUIT FACTORY didn't last very long. I was sacked for not turning up. It wasn't that I didn't like the job. Far from it. I was just sick of working every day only to hand over all of my wages at the end of the week.

So I pretended to be out working. I roamed about the shops in the city centre until the house mother found out and blew her top and made me find another job. By then I was a real pain, her worst nightmare, totally out of control. I did absolutely nothing I was told. Whenever she grounded me or punished me in some other way, I always found a way around it.

On one occasion, she ordered me to peel a huge pot of potatoes as a punishment. So I took the pot out into the garden and filled it with large stones. After peeling just enough potatoes to cover the top of the stones, I put the pot on top of the cooker and walked out. I would have given anything to see the look of horror on the cook's face when she discovered what I'd done.

Another time, the house mother saw me leaving and reminded me I was grounded. It was hard watching the other girls all dressed up and ready to go out with their friends and I was stuck in again. No, I thought, stuff the house mother and her rules. So I put my jacket on to go out.

"You can take that off right now!" the house mother roared, trying to show me she was still in control.

I stared back at her frosty face without flinching, standing my ground. "I'm going out and you're not stopping me."

"You go out that door, I'm calling the police," she snarled.

"Do what you like. I don't care!" I screamed back, slamming the front door behind me on my way out.

This went on for weeks on end. Sometimes I never even bothered going back. I hung about with some of the friends I made at the bowling alley or walked up and down Union Street all night long on my own rather than face the prison warden who showed me not an ounce of kindness or warmth. When the 9 o'clock deadline passed, the house mother always called the police. Many times I was picked up in the small hours of the morning and returned to the hostel.

Despite all the carry ons, I got to know some of the other girls at the hostel quite well. They knew I wasn't flavour of the month with the house mother and I think they felt sorry for me. One night, they invited me to go out with them. I asked them where we were going. But no one in the small group wanted to tell me. I would find out when I got there.

So we put our make-up on and set off. We hadn't walked very far when we reached a pub and I followed them in. The pub was quiet and cosy and I recognised a youth worker who often visited the hostel. He waved at the girls and we went over to where he was sitting and joined him.

"What are you all having to drink?" he said.

I was a little surprised he was buying us drinks because we were all under age. When he asked me what I wanted, I didn't know what to say. The only alcoholic drink I knew was whisky, which I sampled for the first time at a strange party I was invited to. I was working at a local supermarket at the time. It was the only place I could get a job quickly enough after being fired from the biscuit factory. But even that job didn't last long because I kept sleeping in and turning up late.

The party was held in the living room of a flat and most of the people invited were Chinese. There was no dancing or anything like that. The place was in semi-darkness when I entered. A few candles spluttered and flickered and Chinese music played in the background, all adding to the atmosphere. A hazy blue smoke hung in the air making it difficult to see anyone or breathe properly as we all sat in a circle on the floor.

Then a voice said, "Here, have a drink."

A glass of whisky was thrust into my hand. It tasted horrible. But within a minute or two, I started feeling relaxed and began to enjoy myself a little. As my eyes adjusted more and more to the gloom, I spotted an old friend I used to go to school with and he came over and sat down next to me. Andrew was always a polite and well brought up boy, rather square, the last person I expected to see here. I found the party anything but fun and told him I was leaving and he walked me home. He asked me for a date but I didn't fancy him. I didn't want to hurt his feelings either, so I told him I was already seeing someone else.

"I'll have a whisky, please", I blurted out now, not wishing to appear stupid in front of the rest of the girls.

The youth worker's name was Tim, a nice guy and not bad looking either. He was casually dressed with long fair hair falling into curls on his shoulders. Easy to talk to and very relaxed and chilled out, Tim was good company to spend a night out with. He was certainly popular with the other girls as we laughed and chatted away, getting merrier as the evening slipped by.

The girls warned me not to mention Tim or the pub to anyone. It was a secret. They told me the visits to the pub had been going on for quite some time. I felt pleased they trusted me enough to invite me. They saw me now as one of them. I never talked much to Tammy in the hostel. But here, in the relaxed surroundings of the pub, we got on rather well. Tammy was a bubbly redhead who was madly in love with her boyfriend. She was due to meet him shortly at the youth club and invited me to tag along. So we left Tim and the rest of the girls who by this time were a bit worse for wear from the drink.

The youth club was no distance away and Tammy's boyfriend was waiting outside for her. They disappeared together around the back. I went inside and opened the door to the main hall. It was dark although I could see people sitting on chairs in a circle.

"Grab a chair," someone shouted, even though no one knew who I was.

I lifted off a plastic chair from the stack next to the door and joined them. Before I knew it, a large, thick cigarette was passed to me.

"Take a big draw," someone said.

So I did. The smoke hit the back of my throat and my head began to spin. The cigarette left a funny taste in my mouth. My arms and legs started tingling. Nothing seemed real any more. Then someone shouted out the caretaker was due back and everyone scarpered. No one was supposed to be there. That explained why there were no lights on in the hall. Outside, Tammy was nowhere to be seen so I started heading back to the hostel. But the combination of the fresh air, whisky and the cigarette smoke suddenly hit me. I staggered up the road.

When I eventually made it back to the hostel, I found I was locked out. So I rang the doorbell hoping at the same time to keep a sensible head so the house mother wouldn't twig I'd been drinking. I almost got away with it, too. But when I reached the top of the stairs to go to my room, I stumbled and crashed head over heels to the bottom, landing with a thud. Luckily, I was uninjured.

"You've been drinking," the house mother shrieked.

"No I haven't," I replied slowly, slurring my words.

"That's it," she said. "I've had all I can take of you and your behaviour."

"Piss off you fat cow. I've had enough of you, too!" I only just managed to string the sentence together as I picked myself up from the floor.

"Get out of my sight," she yelled.

With that, I turned to face her and blew a huge raspberry. The house mother's jaw dropped in astonishment. Her face turned red with anger. I staggered up the stairs again.

"You've not heard the last of this. Your social worker's going to hear all about it in the morning!"

"Yeah, yeah," I said, her threats having no effect on me whatsoever.

My head hurt the next morning as I struggled to get up and get dressed for work. I was now working at the laundry alongside Sadie who put in a good word for me after I was sacked from the supermarket. I knew I was lucky to get a job there. The job involved washing and pressing hundreds of sheets and pillow cases from hotels all across the city. Sadie was right when she said it was a sweatshop. The heat was incredible from all the different industrial dryers and I never stopped because there were so many sheets to get through in a day. I did have a cigarette break, which I often took out in the fresh air with Sadie, just to get away from the heat and to relax and cool down a bit.

It was during one of these breaks that we hatched a plan to run away to London. Sadie hated the hostel just as much as I did. The idea was to get jobs and to share a flat together. Sadie calculated she had just enough money to get us to Arbroath, but after that we would have to start hitching. We would also have to leave early in the morning in order to get a head start before we were reported missing, so it meant not collecting our wages.

When Friday came, we did everything as if it was just another working day so as not to arouse any suspicion. We left the hostel together and waited at our usual bus stop. But instead of going to work, we got off at the bus station in the city centre. I could hear the excitemenmt in Sadie's voice growing as we boarded the bus for Arbroath. There was no turning back now.

The bus weaved in and out through the morning rush hour traffic and headed south, leaving Aberdeen far behind us. But we paid little attention, sitting in the back of the single-deck bus. We were much too busy talking about London and wondering what it would be like. Neither of us had ever been there and so the thought of it all fired our imaginations. We laughed and cracked jokes and talked about all the things we intended to do. Sadie wanted to find herself a rich husband so she could own a big posh house and drive a flashy car. I wasn't thinking that far ahead.

"Yeah, we'll both find rich husbands and never have to worry about money again," I said, not wanting to spoil Sadie's dream or to show any sign I was feeling a little worried and apprehensive.

By the time the bus arrived and we got off, all the doubts and negative feelings vanished completely. I couldn't quite believe I was back in Arbroath so soon after leaving the place. It felt strange. I desperately wanted to see my friend Elizabeth again. I knew I was taking a bit of a risk going to the hotel where I once worked but I felt it was well worth it.

Little seemed to have changed as I walked inside and spotted her serving guests in the dining room. She was very surprised to see me and told me she was due a break soon, so we agreed to meet in the cafe across the road. Thankfully, there was no sign of Mrs Cameron who would certainly have called the police because she knew I was supposed to be at the hostel.

When Elizabeth walked into the cafe we gave each other a big hug. She looked much more confident than I remembered her. It was so nice to see her doing so well. She told me she was going to be the Camerons' new nanny, and being a kind and caring person, I knew she'd be perfect for the job.

Sadie never said much as she slowly sipped a cup of coffee. It was difficult for her to join in the conversation not knowing anything about my past life in the hotel. I explained to Elizabeth how unhappy I was at the hostel and that I was on the run. She looked worried and concerned and begged me to go back. But I said I was determined to get to London. Nothing or no one was going to stop me and Sadie from getting there.

Elizabeth was due back at the hotel so couldn't stay any longer. I gave her a final hug goodbye and promised to write to her as soon as we made it. After watching her disappear out the door of the cafe, Sadie got up and I followed her into the street. We found a shop and spent the last of our money on crisps and bottles of lemondade and then started walking south along the A92 towards Dundee. We decided to walk instead of hitching it straightaway because we didn't want to draw attention to ourselves. As far as any passing motorists were concerned, we were just two girls out walking along the road. Nothing more. Once we were far enough away, and we judged it was safe enough, then we would try and hitch a lift.

That was the plan. In fact, we ended up walking for the next two days. The road was very long and monotonous and the nights extremely dark and cold. At first we were upbeat, talkative, energetic. There was a spring in our step. It was fun. But the mood changed and we fell silent. We were exhausted. Mile after mile passed by almost in a daze as we placed one foot in front of the other, barely aware of our surroundings. Every time we rested our weary bodies for a few minutes, we wondered if running away was such a good idea after all.

But we finally made it to Dundee. We walked through the city and across the Tay Road Bridge, still following the A92. Two days later, we reached Kirkcaldy, tired out and hungry. The crisps and lemonade which kept us going had long since run out. Now we were arguing and snapping at each other in the middle of the town's never-ending promenade, wondering what to do next.

Then I spotted a ladies' toilet, which was open. So we decided to stay in there overnight and then set off again in the morning. It was anything but luxurious with its cold stone floor. Graffiti covered the walls. But at least it was dry and would keep us out of the wind. Gradually, our strength and spirits revived sitting on the sinks. We read the graffiti out loud and laughed until we almost cried. It wasn't that the graffiti was very funny. It wasn't. We were really laughing at ourselves. There was something crazy about sitting on a sink in a ladies toilet in a strange town reading graffiti off the walls at 2 o'clock in the morning. I think that was what we found really funny. We scribbled on the wall "Pat and Sadie was here" and the date and then fell asleep sitting on a toilet seat.

It was the worst night's sleep I ever had in my life. I twisted and turned, trying to find a comfortable position which proved to be impossible. After managing to doze for a few minutes at a time, I wakened up and then dozed off again. The morning light streaming through the tiny mesh-covered toilet window finally brought the agony to an end. Sadie struggled to move, too, so I knew she'd endured just as bad a few hours as me.

Although we were both glad to get out of there we were still extremely cold and tired. We knew we were in no fit state to walk the next leg of our journey. Looking up and down the length of the promenade, Sadie noticed several parked lorries in the distance which she thought might be heading off at any moment. We should check them out and ask the drivers which direction they were heading and maybe cadge a lift.

"You can ask them," I said, grumpily.

"What's wrong with your face? Get up on the wrong side of the toilet?"

"Ha ha, very funny!" But it did make me crack a smile.

"OK, no bother, I'll ask them."

Off Sadie went to check the lorries out to see if there were any drivers asleep inside. She looked such a tiny figure in the distance, knocking on the cabs and waiting for the windows to roll down. I couldn't help but admire her nerve, but it paid off. Back she ran and I knew we'd struck lucky.

"We can get a lift as far as Queensferry, near the Forth Bridge," she said. "The driver is dropping off his load there. Let's move it."

As we started running over to the lorry, I said, "I'm not sitting next to him in the cab."

"Yes you are. You're sitting next to him. I've done all the asking."

"What if he's a creep?" I said, catching my breath, trying to keep up with Sadie who was a few steps ahead.

"So, it's fine for me to sit next to one?" she added, sounding more and more agitated.

"You're tougher. You'll give him what for, if he tries anything."

Sadie must have thought about it. On reaching the cab, she climbed the step and jumped straight in. I followed and squeezed up next to her and struggled to find the handle to pull the door shut. The driver was in his middle fifties and reminded me of Friar Tuck. His stomach was big and fat and he was balding. He wore a dirty checked shirt and oil-stained jeans.

The driver never told us his name and I didn't feel like asking him either. Judging by her expression, Sadie was as wary of him as I was. I was glad she was sitting next to him and not me. Several miles passed by before our instincts were proved to be correct. At first, the driver was chatty, trying his best to engage us in some trivial conversation.

"Where are you girls heading for?"

"London," said Sadie.

"Got family there, have you?"

"Yes."

Silence. A few seconds later, the driver tried again.

"So where have you come from?"

"Visiting my gran in Inverurie."

"You've come a long way then," said the driver, not believing a word of it.

Sadie was determined not to give the game away. So we sat silently, staring out at the empty road ahead. There were hardly any cars about because it was still very early. The driver tried once more.

"Your friend's a bit quiet?"

"Sorry, I'm just a little bit tired," I replied.

The cab was beginning to warm up and I felt relaxed, enjoying the heat. I must have dozed off. The next thing I knew Sadie was screaming and swearing at the driver, demanding he stop the lorry immediately or she would get the police on to him. I didn't know what was happening. I was terrified.

"Stop the lorry!" Sadie shouted again, almost in the driver's ear.

It was obvious she was frightened, too, but she was also angry and determined to stand up to him. So the verbal onslaught continued. It worked. The driver had second thoughts and as he slammed on the brakes, the lorry came to a screeching halt.

"Get out! Piss off the both of you!" the driver snarled.

I fumbled for the door handle and jumped out as fast as I could. Sadie followed me just as quickly.

"Whew, that was a lucky escape," I said.

Sadie was in shock and shaking with rage. "Creep!" she roared out. "Dirty perv!" She was still shouting for all she was worth as the lorry disappeared down the road. "I'm getting the police on you. You're not getting away with it you big fat creep!"

When she calmed down enough, I asked her what happened. "I fell asleep," I said, feeling a bit guilty.

"The bastard tried it on."

Sadie looked at me, and never mentioned any more about it again. We were now in North Queensferry, a pretty little village dominated by the Forth Rail Bridge. The bridge was massive, impressive, but I'd only ever seen it on biscuit tins before. Now I was standing right below it, looking up as it streaked out across the River Forth. It was an unforgettable sight. Visible in the distance was the Forth Road Bridge. We knew we'd have no option but to walk across it.

"I'm starving," we both blurted out at exactly the same moment.

We laughed. Sadie was getting back to her old self again. I was pleased for her.

After pausing, she said, "Notice the rolls and milk?"

"Where?"

"On the doorsteps!"

Before I knew it, she bounded off into the nearest garden. A few moments later she came back, clutching a bottle of milk and rolls. "Let's get out of here quick!" she said.

We walked smartly in the direction of the road bridge until we were far enough away. Then we stopped and scoffed the lot. After having so little to eat for days, the rolls tasted heavenly and we felt so much happier.

"I fancy looking at the city centre in Edinburgh, looking at some of the shops," I said.

"Good idea. Why don't we?" said Sadie.

But I realised we both looked like a couple of tramps after being on the run for days. Having brought no clean clothes to change into wasn't very sensible planning on our part. We didn't even

have a comb with us to tidy our hair. There was nothing we could
do about it now except enjoy the spectacular view from hundreds
of feet up as we walked slowly across the bridge. The pedestrian
and cycle path seemed to go on for ever. But at least we were safe,
separated from the cars and lorries now whizzing past north and
south, heading for the Fife coast or to Edinburgh. After what
seemed like an age we made it to the other side. We were glad just
to be out of the strong winds which suddenly appeared from
nowhere and which dogged our every step. But there was no wind
now as we followed the cycle path, unsure of what to do next. We
certainly never noticed the police patrol car which quietly
sneaked up behind us.

"Where might you ladies be going?" said a commanding voice
suddenly, stopping us dead in our tracks.

We turned around. A few feet away from us stood a tall policeman. I knew we had to think fast. Sadie jumped in before me.

"We're going to my aunty's house," she said.

"So where does she live?"

"Queensferry," Sadie replied, trying to sound confident.

"Where about?"

"Marchmount Crescent."

It was the first name she thought of. The policeman smiled.
"Sorry ladies, no such address. Get in the car."

There was nothing we could do. The game was well and truly up.
We sat silently in the back of the police car which was now taking us
to the nearest police station. I was terrified at the thought of the
trouble we were in. What was going to happen to us?

At the police station we were booked in and after confirming
our names and addresses one of the policemen went off and made
a few telephone calls. He came back a few minutes later, satisfied
we were indeed who we said we were. We were also the missing
girls half the police forces in Scotland were looking for.

"You know you were on the news and in the papers?"

"Fame at last," I said, laughing.

But I was amazed, too, that our little escapade had caused such a stir across the country. The policemen were very nice to us and offered us sandwiches and cups of tea. We were really grateful because we were still starving. A short time afterwards, we were driven to separate hostels in Edinburgh. The hostel I was taken to was friendly and homely and the lady who ran it was kind and warm and really cared about the girls under her care. I asked her if I could live at the hostel permanently but she said it wasn't allowed. Disappointed, I made my way upstairs and had a long, relaxing bath then caught up on some much needed sleep.

Early next morning, shortly after breakfast, a young smartly dressed man in a dark suit appeared unexpectedly. He told me to stick my hand out. Then he snapped one end of a pair of handcuffs around my wrist and the other around his. I was led out the hostel to a waiting car.

"We're taking you to the airport and flying you back to Aberdeen," he said. That was all he said. There was no further explanation as we sat in the back of a car heading towards the airport. I couldn't believe what was happening. It was a shock. This was the first time I'd ever been handcuffed and it made me feel like a common criminal. The young man was so matter-of-fact about it all, cold and clinical, as if I was some lump of meat to be pushed and shoved wherever he wanted.

The silence continued throughout the short journey. The young man never talked or made any effort to be friendly. When we arrived at the airport he pulled me out the car and up the stairs into a passenger plane. Without speaking, he motioned me to sit down. Within a minute, Sadie, too, was sitting handcuffed on the plane, a few seats further back from me. The other passengers knew nothing of what was going on. We sat tucked up next to the window out of sight. As we took off, I realised this was the first time I'd ever been on a plane. It was exciting watching the ground disappear and then being up amongst the clouds. I felt all my troubles were left behind on the ground, somewhere far below. But the feeling didn't last long. When we touched down, I knew I was being returned to a place I hated, where there was no love or warmth.

Mrs Strachan was waiting for me at the bottom of the stairs when I stepped out of the plane. I was glad to be shot of the young man and his handcuffs. After being ushered into a waiting car I was driven to the hostel. I said nothing to Mrs Strachan during the short drive to the hostel. The house mother dived straight out the front door the moment we pulled up and her cold eyes stared hard at me. Her arms were tightly folded over her puffed-out chest. It was obvious she was dying to have a go at me.

"Who do you think you are, running away?" she growled. "Get inside, now!"

Looking hard at Mrs Strachan, I said, "You put me back in there and I'll be gone by the end of the week. There's no way I'm staying with that witch!"

My words were aimed squarely at Mrs Strachan and not the house mother, who by now was used to my hostility. I'd thrown down the gauntlet, determined once and for all to make a stand. Now I hoped Mrs Strachan would pick it up. Thankfully, she did.

"Are you that unhappy living here?" she asked.

"Yes!" I snapped.

"You can hate it all you like," said the house mother. "It doesn't change anything. Get inside."

"Patricia, get back in the car."

The house mother looked stunned.

"If Patricia is so unhappy here then she doesn't have to stay," said Mrs Strachan. "Get back in the car Patricia."

I could hardly believe it. Did she really say I didn't have to live there any more? In that moment, I knew it was Mrs Strachan who had the real power and not the house mother. The house mother stood rooted to the spot, speechless, her mouth wide open. As we drove away, I summoned up the cheekiest widest grin I was capable of. I wanted her to know I was the winner and she had lost the battle. If only I'd known, my moment of triumph was to be a very short-lived one indeed.

Chapter Seventeen

MY HEART SANK as I looked at the bright yellow painted walls. This was a place of no escape. There were no normal windows here through which to look at the outside world. They were set high up in the walls, allowing only the tiniest glimpse of the sky and clouds through thick steel bars. I was confused. Why had Mrs Strachan dumped me here? It was a place meant for young offenders. Was she even coming back for me? Climbing the stairs on the way to the room allocated to me, I had no answers to the questions spinning around in my head. I felt completely abandoned.

My room was painted the same ghastly yellow colour as everywhere else. It was so small it felt more like a cell. Most of the little space available was taken up by a single bed. I still had no clean clothes to change into or any to put in the tiny wooden chest of drawers next to it. I sat down on the bed not knowing what to do with myself. Since my arrival here, the only person I'd seen was a young lad coming down the stairs as I went up them. He seemed to be in a rush to go somewhere and never uttered a word or even turned his head to look at me. I wondered what happened to Sadie and hoped she was all right, wherever she was.

But I needn't have worried. A few minutes later, I heard the heavy door to the place click open and rushed out my room to have a look. Standing alone at the bottom of the stairs was Sadie. Instantly, I felt cheered up and shouted down to her. But there was no smile of recognition as she climbed the stairs onto the landing and stopped in front of me.

"What's wrong?" I said.

"I'm only here for one night and my social worker's coming for me tomorrow. They're going to dump me in some other hostel."

"At least you know you're going somewhere else and not staying here," I said. "It might be all right. You might like it. Can't be any worse than the last place."

"Not much I can do about it anyway."

As she shrugged and hunched her shoulders, I knew something inside her was changed. Her eyes were empty and distant, as if focused on something far away. This was not the Sadie I knew, who always laughed and joked whenever things were bad. It was plain she wasn't in the mood for talking much. She made an excuse about being tired and walked off to her room only a few doors along from mine, shutting me and the rest of the world out.

I was overcome by a deep sense of sadness and despair. Back in my room, I just lay on my bed and stared at the ceiling for hours on end. There was nothing else to do. I had nothing to read and no radio and there was no television room I could go to either, nothing to occupy my mind. When I got up early next morning, Sadie was gone. We never had the chance to say goodbye. I never saw her again. Many years later, I heard she married a soldier. But I don't know if that was true or not.

At the end of another long and dreary day, I was summoned to appear before the lady who ran the place. Not knowing quite what to expect, I was a little surprised when the member of staff who came for me then led me through to her living room. The lady was sitting near a roaring fire reading a report, surrounded by paperwork. She was in her middle forties and her black shiny hair was shaped neatly into a Swiss roll at the back. Her eyes lifted from the report and looked directly at me as I stood nervously waiting for her to say something.

"I'm puzzled," she finally said. "Why are you here?"

I shrugged my shoulders because I didn't know myself.

"As far as I can see, all you've done is run away. You've got no criminal record. You've done nothing wrong to bring you here." She paused for a moment, thinking, before shaking her head. "No no no! This is wrong. You shouldn't have been brought here. I'm getting this sorted out immediately."

She looked very cross and concerned, as if realising I'd been dumped by a system that only wanted to wash their hands of me. She was having none of it and promised to contact Mrs Strachan first thing in the morning to find somewhere else more suitable for me to go. "Don't worry. We'll have this all cleared up tomorrow."

With that, I was dismissed. As I walked back to my room, I felt an overwhelming sense of relief. With a bit of luck, I'd soon be out of here, away from this miserable place. True to her word, Mrs Strachan arrived to collect me the next day to take me to another hostel. In the car on the way there, she asked me when was the last time I visited a hairdresser. My hair looked such a mess. I said, when I was 10, and she looked rather surprised. My dishevelled appearance also caused my new house mother some concern, too, judging by the expression of horror on her face.

The house mother was small and plump with rosy cheeks and silvery hair and turned out to be a much kinder lady. She welcomed me and hoped I would be happy in my new home. More for reassurance than anything else, Mrs Strachan made a point of telling her she was going to arrange a hairdresser's appointment for me. And she would be using social work funds to buy me some new clothes, too. She explained how at the last hostel I was given no money out of my wages to buy clothes or anything else.

My new room looked much the same as the last one, with the same familiar layout, three beds taking up most of the space. Instead of small, individual chests of drawers, there was one large sliding wardrobe, which was shared. But, of course, the few posessions I owned were still at the last hostel and hadn't yet been sent on. All I had was the clothes I stood up in, and they were now badly in need of a wash. My room-mates came from Edinburgh and Fraserburgh. They never told me the circumstances which brought them to the hostel, so far away from their homes. I had the feeling the hostel was for girls who had been in some kind of trouble. Later, my initial suspicions were proved to be correct. My room-mates warned me two or three of the girls were real trouble makers and not to cross them.

"Watch your back," said Margaret, the girl from Edinburgh. "Be careful what you say. Some of them don't need any excuse to pick a fight."

The contrast between me and Mrs Strachan, who was always immaculately turned out, was plainly obvious as I stepped out her car and headed towards a rather posh department store in the middle of town. I was eagerly looking forward to some new clothes, even though I had no real idea what I wanted to wear. Mrs Strachan saw I was struggling to make my mind up. I didn't have much of a clue about fashion. So she gently made a few suggestions as to what would look nice. She picked up a purple woollen maxi coat for me to try on. I felt it was much too elegant for someone like me. But I didn't want to hurt her feelings either.

"That's lovely and warm," I said.

"Right, we'll take it," she told the shop assistant standing next to her.

For the next couple of hours I tried on all kinds of clothes, from dresses and shoes to jumpers and underwear. Every time I liked something, Mrs Strachan bought it. I don't know how much money she actually spent on me. It was a lot. We were both weighed down with bags filled to the brim when we finally left the department store. After locking the clothes away in the boot of her car, she took me to the hairdresser for my appointment.

When I eventually arrived back at the hostel I lovingly slipped each new item of clothing onto a wooden coat hanger, enjoying the look and feel and texture of each for a moment before hanging it up in the wardrobe. I was particularly proud of the long silk maxi dress with matching hot pants. This was one of the best days of my life.

For the first time in a very long time I felt really good about myself. I quickly settled into the routine of the hostel and got myself a job in a fish factory. It wasn't the greatest of jobs. I stood for hours in front of a steel table packing prawns into white plastic containers after first cracking and pulling off their hard shells. It was cold and wet but at least the wages were reasonable. The women either side of me were friendly and chatty which helped to break the monotony of each long day.

I caught a teenage boy looking at me all the time and at the end of the first week, he asked me out on a date. We arranged to go dancing in the Douglas Hotel. But he turned up high as a kite, hardly able to string a sentence together. So I left in disgust. I was not going to go out with anyone who took drugs. He never asked me out again.

When I returned to the hostel after a hard day in the fish factory, my room-mate Margaret warned me someone was going into the wardrobe and helping themselves to my clothes. I was furious.

"What a bloody cheek! Who's doing it?" I demanded angrily.

"Martha Stewart. Look, watch it, though. She's got a reputation for fighting."

"I don't bloody care. She's not helping herself to my stuff!" By now I was boiling mad, itching to confront her. She was not getting away with it, no matter what sort of reputation she had. I tracked her down to the dining room and let fly.

"I hear you've been helping yourself to my clothes when I'm at work!"

"So what!" she fired back.

She was skinny looking, with mousy brown collar-length hair. Although at least a year or more older than me, she didn't look that tough.

"You'd better not be wearing my clothes again," I roared out, barely six inches from her face.

"Or you'll do what?" she snarled back.

Suddenly, she pulled away and grabbed a chair from the dining table. With a look of menace on her face, she waved it slowly in front of me, moving it from side to side, trying to intimidate me.

"You don't frighten me!" I said, holding my ground.

"Oh, don't I?" she spat out, moving a little closer.

Without warning, Martha threw the chair down and launched herself at me. There was no option but to defend myself. I punched and kicked her and grabbed her hair which came out in handfuls. We fell to the floor, rolling and twisting, scratching and biting and lashing out at every opportunity. But neither of us was able to gain the upper hand.

Somehow, Martha managed to wriggle free, grabbing hold of the upturned chair as she did so. She struggled to her feet and raised it above her head ready to slam down on me. But I was already one step ahead of her with a chair of my own. I swung it from behind me and then launched it full force towards her body. It caught her smack in the middle of the hip. She let out a cry of pain.

Alerted by the noise, the house mother and two members of

staff came charging through and immediately jumped to all the wrong conclusions. Martha turned on the tears and played the victim for all she was worth. I was hauled through to the house mother's sitting room where I found myself having to defend my actions.

"We've never had girls behaving like this before," the house mother fumed.

"But it wasn't my fault. She was going into my wardrobe and taking my clothes out," I tried to explain.

The house mother was having none of it. "Silence! Martha's never been in any trouble since she's lived here," she said. "You've only been here a short time and there's all this trouble."

I knew it was hopeless. Anything I said would only fall on deaf ears.

"No. We'll have to get you removed from here. We don't tolerate this kind of disruptive behaviour. It's not fair on the rest of the girls. I'll be talking to your social worker. I want you out of here."

With that, I was told to go. Later on, lying on my bed, I realised why there had never been any trouble here before. The rest of the girls were too frightened to stand up to Martha. So they let her get away with all her bullying. Mrs Strachan turned up the next day and she was anything but pleased to see me.

"What am I meant to do with you?" she asked.

I had no answer, so I said nothing. I could see she now thought me a hopeless case.

"What do you want me to do to help you?" Mrs Strachan was at her wits' end, her patience all but run out.

"Get me out of hostels," I said. "I just want to be on my own. Why can't I get another live-in job?"

Mrs Strachan thought hard for a moment, surprised by my answer. But it was worth considering, judging by her expression. She told me to pack my belongings and then we were off again, on the way to her office. We drove through the city streets in silence. I knew Mrs Strachan must have been mulling over the options. When we arrived, I was invited to sit down. Then she excused herself, saying she had a few telephone calls to make. When she returned, there was a look of satisfaction on her face.

"I've managed to get you a live-in job at the university, waitressing," she announced.

I discovered later I only got the job because the manageress at Aberdeen University was a personal friend. She was doing Mrs Strachan a favour. I moved into a small single room next to the halls of residence and started work the following day. The job wasn't hard. All I had to do was serve the students breakfast, lunch and evening meal, clear away the tables and sweep the floor. For the first time, I was allowed to keep all my wages to myself, which meant I could buy new clothes and tops and other bits and pieces. I had my own key to come and go as I liked and was free to make my own decisions. This was all I ever wanted.

I started going dancing at the Palais de Danse. You had to be 18 to get in. But when I put my make-up on, I looked much older. So I never had a problem getting through the doors. I loved the atmosphere and the people I met, the noise and the hustle and bustle of a packed Friday and Saturday night. I wore hot pants and high platform shoes which were all the fashion. A huge revolving mirror globe hung from the ceiling, sending patterns of light streaming across the dance floor. Freda Payne's "Band of Gold" or "Chirpy Chirpy Cheep Cheep" by Middle of the Road or Lynn Anderson's "I Never Promised You a Rose Garden" were at the top of the charts.

The boys came over and chatted me up and danced with me, but at that time I wasn't interested in having a boyfriend. I was more into drinking Blue Lagoons and getting drunk and staggering back to the halls of residence in the small hours of the morning. As a result, I often slept in and was late for work, rushing down to find breakfast already over and the other waitresses clearing away the plates. I didn't blame them for throwing me dirty looks.

The halls of residence were usually packed with students from all over the country. They chose to study in Aberdeen because of the university's excellent reputation. I became particularly friendly with two student girls from Glasgow, both in their late teens. They were struggling to make ends meet on a meagre budget. Although they never stayed in the halls, they came to the dining room for meals.

They invited me back to their flat which was in a rough part of Aberdeen. I felt sorry for them having to live in such a run-down area. But they couldn't afford anywhere else. They were such nice girls, too. We climbed the dingy stairs of the tenement block to the top landing. Just as were were about to enter the flat, they popped next door to their neighbour's flat, to see if they could borrow some money and milk. They entered without knocking, so I figured they must know their neighbour well and be on really friendly terms.

I followed them through to a small sparsely furnished living room which hadn't seen a paintbrush in many years. The paper on the walls was faded and torn in places and the dirty red carpet had seen better days. The room felt cold and smelled of damp. I sat down on an old battered settee in front of an empty hearth choked by cinders and ash. Standing with his back to me was a young man. He was staring at himself in the large mirror hanging above the fireplace. I let out a quiet gasp as I recognised the reflection.

It was Jack, the councillor's son, the young kid who'd gone crazy one school dinnertime causing a riot. I never trusted him then and I didn't trust him now. But I said nothing. He turned around with no sign of acknowledgement and announced he was going to get changed in the bedroom.

The students whispered amongst themselves, trying to decide who would ask for the money and milk when he returned. I didn't mention I knew him from long ago as we listened to him pacing up and down in the bedroom, muttering to himself. The tension grew. We sat silently looking at each other, waiting for the bedroom door to open again.

But it wasn't Jack who appeared, finally, but someone else, an alter ego complete with blonde wig, heavy make-up, flowery figure-hugging dress, high heels and stockings. I was totally freaked out and wanted to run as far away as I could but managed with the greatest of effort not to say anything or show any reaction. Jack walked past me and over to the mirror again, puffing and pouting his bright ruby-red lips to make sure the lipstick hadn't stained his pearly white front teeth. Next he checked his large false eyelashes and separated and straightened out one or two lashes clogged up by the black mascara surrounding his heavily made-up eyes.

Looking rather satisfied with himself after giving his body profile the once over, Jack turned to look at us. The students sat open mouthed, dumbfounded, in a state of shock, with thoughts of money and milk the last thing on their minds. He went over to the side of the settee and picked up a black shiny patent leather handbag.

Then he paused for a moment, staring at the students, enjoying their obvious discomfort, and said in a lady-like voice, "Don't call me Jack any more. My name is Rosie. See yourselves out darlings. I'm off."

We listened in silence as the sound of Rosie's high heels clicked and echoed in the tenement stairway. She made her way down to the bottom floor and then out into the street. I dashed over to the window not really believing she would have the nerve to walk out dressed like that. But she did. She moved along the street in a rather unsteady manner, gripping the handbag tightly to her body, managing somehow not to stumble or fall flat on her face, until she disappeared out of view. The students spent the night sitting in their flat in the dark with neither milk for tea or money to feed the electric meter. I made my way back to the university determined never to set foot in Jack's flat again.

⁂

It was years since I last saw my sister Lottie and now I had the chance to track her down and build up the relationship we should have had all along but for the interference of the authorities. She was family and I needed her to be part of my life. From kids at school, I knew the name of the housing estate my mother and father lived in. I didn't want to talk to them because my emotions were still too raw, but the area was a good starting point in the quest for my sister. So I started knocking on doors and eventually someone told me they knew her and where she lived.

Late one Saturday afternoon, I turned up at her door. She was heavily pregnant with her second child, David. It hardly seemed five years had passed since we last met. I knew she was married but I wasn't allowed to go to the wedding. She smiled and invited me inside. We sat in the living room drinking cups of tea and reminiscing, making up for all the lost years.

I popped in to see her regularly over the coming weeks, sometimes staying over the weekend if I wasn't going out dancing. Returning back to the university one Sunday, I discovered to my horror I had forgotten to take the plug out of the sink and to turn off the tap. Water overflowed and soaked the carpets and seeped out through the bottom of door and into the corridor. When the alarm was raised the caretaker used a spare key to get into my room. But it was too late. The damage was done.

The carpets were soaking wet and had to be thrown out. The manageress was fed up with me always sleeping in and now had the excuse she was looking for. So she fired me. Once again, Mrs Strachan got an unexpected telephone call. By the time she came to collect me, she had already made arrangements for me to stay at the YWCA at the Spital in Old Aberdeen. The YWCA was barely a stone's throw from the children's home I left less than a year before. This was my fifth move since then and the stress of it all was beginning to tell. I was sinking into depression.

The YWCA was a cold and friendless place, where I slept most days until dinner time. The lady in charge grew sick of me always lying in bed and often came through and started shouting at me, calling me a lazy good-for-nothing. I should be ashamed of myself, she said, but I didn't care about other people's opinion of me.

I couldn't shake myself out of the lethargy which left me with little enthusiasm for life. Mrs Strachan wanted to take me to the doctor because she was convinced I needed iron tablets. She stopped being disappointed in me and started to take a real interest in my welfare, sometimes giving me one of her jumpers because my room was so cold, and running me in her car to job interviews.

Doreen, who was several years older than me, lived in the room next to mine and asked me one afternoon if I'd like to come shopping in the city centre for something to do. I jumped at the chance. We went into Marks and Spencer admiring all the different dresses and outfits on display. Taking one or two off the racks, she held them against her smallish frame and asked me if they suited her and if I liked the colour. I said I did and then she went to try on some blouses, making comments every so often.

"That blouse makes me look too fat," she said, emerging from the changing room and pressing me for my opinion.

"You're anything but fat," I replied. "You're a twig. I wish I was as skinny as you."

My weight had shot up since leaving the children's home and I was struggling to shift the extra pounds. Satisfied with the clothes she picked, Doreen headed over to the counter to pay for them.

The smartly dressed assistant said, "Will madam be paying by cash or cheque?"

"By cheque," replied Doreen.

She wrote out a cheque to pay for the goods which came to quite a lot of money. With a rather smug look on her face, Doreen turned to me and said, "Fancy going to the pub?"

Not realising you could get a drink in the afternoon, I told her I had no money.

"Don't worry about that. We'll go over to the bank across the road and cash a cheque."

I stood outside the bank and waited for her to return.

"See, no problem!" she said, waving a £20 note in her hand, which was a small fortune.

I was beginning to wonder where all the money was coming from for I knew she didn't have a job. We arrived back at the YWCA a few hours later, feeling rather merry after downing a good few vodka and oranges at a grotty little pub around the corner from the bank. I went to my room to sleep off the effects and a short time later an argument between Doreen and her room-mate Cathy brought me to my senses.

"No, it's nothing like that!"

"Then you tell me what the hell is going on!" thundered back Cathy. "Get out the way. I'm phoning the police!"

The door slammed shut and the room fell silent. I went back to sleep. I was suddenly awakened again, this time by the loud sound of banging on my room door. Half awake, I opened it to see two policemen and before I had the chance to ask what they wanted, they told me to come down to the police station to answer a few questions.

"What's going on?" I said.

"Just come with us. We need you to help us with our enquiries."

I still wasn't any the wiser sitting in the back of the police car being driven to the police station. I was ushered into a little room where two detectives were sitting waiting for me. I confirmed my name and address and then one of them asked me if I had stolen the chequebook belonging to Catherine Simpson.

"No. I've not stolen anything," I said, looking puzzled and feeling a little frightened.

"Did you go out with with Doreen Skinner this afternoon?"

"Yes," I replied, but before I could explain further, he fired off another question.

"Did you use the chequebook to buy items of clothing?"

"No, no, it was Doreen," I replied in a nervous, faltering voice. "I didn't know it was stolen. I thought it was hers."

More questions followed until they seemed satisfied I was completely innocent and I was driven back to the YWCA. By this time I was boiling mad, looking to confront Doreen for dragging me into such a situation. I thumped hard on her door but Cathy refused to open it, shouting Doreen was at the police station, not in the room. There was no answer either when I knocked the following day, still feeling angry over the whole affair. A resident seeing me knocking asked me what was wrong. When I told her what happened, she told me Cathy had dropped all the charges.

"Why, when she stole her chequebook? Why would she let her away with it?"

The resident laughed. "You must be the only one here who doesn't know. They're lovers, lesbians."

I was amazed. I never knew there was such a thing, a woman loving another woman. But it explained everything, how Cathy had jumped to the wrong conclusion when I went out with Doreen, shopping. She was jealous of me. And that's why they were arguing after we returned from the pub. She wanted to get her own back and lied to the police about the chequebook to get her into trouble, even although she'd given her permission to use it. Now, I felt, she was out to get rid of me, although I didn't know what her plan was until a little later. Personal items started disappearing out the rooms. At the same time, she began to spread rumours pointing the finger at me and saying I was not to be trusted.

It all came to a head when I returned from my sister's house. The girl I shared my room with warned me the girls in the hostel had plans to beat me up. She told me to be on my guard. They were deadly serious. I knew it was true because they'd been giving me the cold shoulder for days. Whenever I tried to talk to any of them, they ignored me, so I knew something was going on.

Now I needed help. The only thing I could think of was to telephone Margaret, a friend I went out dancing with. I asked her to go over to my sister's house to tell her to get here fast. Margaret sounded worried and promised she would. Then she'd be over herself with Lottie. But they arrived too late.

A group of girls were already hiding in the foyer, listening, waiting until I finished telephoning. They followed me as I made my way up the stairs to my room. At the same time, another group of girls suddenly appeared at the top of the stairs. I was cornered, trapped like a rat on the small landing in the middle, unable to go up or down. The ringleader was Trish, a fat blonde girl, who a few days ago wanted to borrow my silk dress and matching hot pants. I knew she would have struggled to fit into them, so I said no. It wasn't the answer she was looking for. Now it was payback time. She looked down at me, menacingly, trying to intimidate me with her weight and height, egging the other girls on.

I was frightened. There seemed no way out. Suddenly, a voice inside my head boomed out, Faint! I obeyed instantly, without thinking, and flopped to the floor, banging my head on the cold stone landing. As I pretended to be unconscious, with my eyes shut, I heard them panicking and blaming each other.

"I knew this was wrong, so stupid," said one girl, angrily.

"Oh God, is she OK?" screamed another.

A third girl rounded on Trish, shouting at the top of her voice, "It's all your fault, it's all your fault!"

All thoughts of beating me up vanished. The girls were full of regrets and the recriminations were flying up and down the stairs. They argued amongst themselves, unable to decide what to do next. Then I felt someone shaking me, calling my name, hitting me gently on the face, trying to bring me round. I still kept up the pretence even although the back of my head was throbbing. After a few seconds, I slowly opened my eyes. Two girls helped me to my feet. Then they supported me under each arm and guided me slowly up the stairs to my room and onto my bed.

Just at that moment Lottie and Margaret walked into the room, pushing their way through the the girls crowding around my bed, ready to have a go at them. But the girls were now appologising profusely, trying hard to make amends. Lottie told them all to get out and they quickly disappeared. Only Trish remained. This was my opportunity. There was no way I was letting her off with this. Before she realised what was happening, I was out my bed and on my feet. I grabbed her clothes and twisted them around her neck, shoving her hard up against the wall.

"You ever try that again and I'll put your head right through this wall," I screamed out, inches from her face.

Now the boot was on the other foot. There were no friends to hide behind. She looked petrified as I gripped her even more tightly, choking the life out of her. I had no intentions of beating her up or doing her any real harm. I just wanted to give her a taste of her own medicine. She was off the moment I loosened my grip, running out the room like a scared witless rabbit. But my moment of triumph was short-lived. In stormed the YWCA manageress, ranting and raving. Not only was I a good-for-nothing. I was also a troublemaker and she wasn't having my sort living here.

"I want you out, tomorrow. I'll be phoning your social worker."

Sure enough, Mrs Strachan turned up the next day with no smile to greet me. There was only silence between us as she watched me packing up my belongings. The silence continued as we drove back to her office once again. I never made any effort to explain what happened. There was no point. I don't think she would have believed me anyway. Everyone assumed I was the guilty party. The silence was finally broken.

"I'm at my wits' end with you. I've nowhere else to put you," she snapped. "The only place left is an approved school, in Glasgow. Is that what you want?"

"No."

"What do you want me to do with you?" Mrs Strachan sat hunched over her desk, her head between her hands. She looked ground down, bereft of ideas, at the end of her tether.

"No more hostels, no more social workers, no more, no more, I've had enough!" I cried out. "I just want to be on my own."

My outburst took her completely by surprise and she sat straight up. It was as if she was suddenly transformed, energised, a different person all of a sudden. "Is that what you really want?"

"Yes," I said, emphatically.

Mrs Strachan thought for a moment.

"Right, if you can prove to me you can get a job, and keep it for a month, and not get into any kind of trouble, I'll set up a children's panel and see if we can get you removed from care. Would that make you happy?"

"Yes," I said, nodding enthusiastically.

"But first we need to get you somewhere to live."

"It's OK," I reassured her. "My friend Margaret's mum will let me stay with them."

"If you're sure, then that's all right with me."

Margaret's mum was a lovely woman and had no problems offering me a place to stay. I took the first job I found, which was in another fish factory. Even although I didn't much like it, I stuck it out. I made sure I kept my nose clean and avoided anything which might land me in trouble. It felt like a breath of fresh air living in a normal family atmosphere, something I'd never known before. This certainly helped me feel so much better about myself.

Mrs Strachan appeared bright and early on the day of the panel hearing. She explained in detail what was to happen and how best to behave. I waited outside nervously until I was called in and told to sit down. There were a dozen people seated around a long oval table, men dressed smartly in suits and also several well-dressed ladies. They were all reading copies of a report containing everything about me, my life history, stretching back to the very first home I was brought up in.

An elderly man addressed me. He reminded me of a minister with his holier-than-thou attitude. "Where are you living now?" he asked.

"At my friend's mum's house," I answered back.

"I see you're working. Are you sticking the job?"

"Yes," I answered meekly.

He turned a few pages of the report and muttered to himself. He seemed to be in charge of the panel.

"You've never been in any trouble with the police?"

"No, sir."

"It's very important you keep your job and make something of your life," he said.

The other panel members nodded. That was about as much as they contributed to the proceedings.

Looking around the table, he added, "If we're all in agreement, I believe there's no reason for Patricia continuing to be in care."

The rest of the panel murmured their approval and the meeting was closed. I was free, at last, amazed by the power wielded by these unknown faceless people who neither knew me or had ever met me before. Mrs Strachan was so happy for me and relieved to be no longer responsible for my welfare. She suggested going to the pub to celebrate but forgot for a moment I had only just turned 16.

Chapter Eighteen

I THINK I HATED DUNDEE the moment I stepped off the bus. Maybe it had something to do with being back in the city so soon after running away. I remembered how exhausted and hungry I felt as I walked with Sadie through the streets. The memory was still raw.

It was dark and raining hard and I had no idea where I was going. All I had with me was my battered brown suitcase and a few shillings in my purse and the name of the street where my mum and dad lived. It was my sister Lottie who suggested I go and live with them after telling me they were now staying in Dundee, but I can't say I was keen on the idea. There were too many painful memories to confront. The thought of living with two strangers who were alcoholics filled me with dread.

I was over the moon after the children's panel hearing. But I was also a little scared. Now there was no one to bail me out if things went wrong. Quickly, I dismissed such negative thoughts and wasted no time saying goodbye to Mrs Strachan. I headed back to Margaret's house where her mum looked shocked as she watched me throw my belongings into my case.

After only a few minutes my case was packed and I thanked her and was off. I knew she expected me to stay with her, but there was no way I was going to hang about, just in case I landed back in care again. I wanted to get as far away from Aberdeen as I could, so I borrowed some money from Lottie. There was enough for the ticket to Dundee and a little bit left over.

I jumped into the first taxi I saw and pulled out the crumpled piece of paper Lottie gave me with the name of the street Mum and Dad lived in. The taxi stopped at the top of the street a few minutes later. The middle-aged taxi driver sounded nervous.

"Lass, I'm not happy dropping you off here in the middle of the night, knocking on doors," he said.

"I'll be all right."

"Look at the state of the place."

I had to agree. The street was dimly lit with run-down tenements rising either side from deep dark shadows. Some had their windows smashed in and others were boarded up. It made me feel uneasy.

"Look, I'll take you to the police station. They'll give you a bed for the night. I think it's best. They might be able to trace your parents' house in the morning."

The driver was right. I nodded in agreement. He drove me to Bell Street police station. After making sure I would be put up in a cell for the night, he wished me the best of luck in my search. I thanked him and he left, leaving me in the hands of the duty policeman who showed me to the cell and locked me in. The cell was small and bare except for a hard wooden bed with a thin mattress on top. It wasn't comfortable but at least I was safe. I fell asleep as soon as I lay down.

The same policeman appeared in the morning carrying a mug of hot steaming tea and a plate of porridge. I was starving. I hadn't eaten anything for more than twelve hours. He was friendly and cheery and told me he'd phoned up the Salvation Army and they had a place for me to stay. He said the taxi driver had also left £20 to help me until I got myself sorted out. He handed me the money.

It was a small fortune in those days. I felt overwhelmed by such kindness from a complete stranger. The policeman said he had come across my mum and dad before and advised me to leave well alone. It wasn't a good idea me going to see them. He pointed me in the direction of the Salvation Army hostel, which was just up the road from the station.

The first thing I noticed entering the large old-fashioned three-storey building was how neat and spotless everything was. It was modern looking and clinical, but the place lacked any homely touches. The shiny wooden floor was so clean you could eat your dinner off of it. Lists of rules jumped out at you from everywhere you looked. I walked through to the dining room where a young mum was spoon-feeding a small child. There were lots of homeless old ladies milling around, complaining amongst themselves about getting kicked out for the day. I felt sorry for them all. They filed past me out the building to wander the streets aimlessly until 5 o'clock. Only then would they be allowed inside again for some warmth and shelter.

My room was as neat and tidy as the rest of the hostel. I shared it with Jan, a chatty and friendly girl who was a little bit older than me. She invited me the next day to her boyfriend's flat, which was on the first floor of a tenement block in the Downfield area in the north of the city. Mick, her boyfriend, answered the door and we went inside.

They left me sitting alone in the living room while they disappeared into the bedroom. I couldn't help but hear the moans and groans and the squeaking of bedsprings as I sat there, in the quiet, feeling very embarrassed. I didn't expect anything like that. When the love-making session was over, they both came through. Mick tried to make conversation with me. I disliked him straight away. All my instincts told me he was trouble. Despite my feelings, I was friendly enough towards him so as not to offend Jan. After the two of them made arrangements to meet again the following day, they said goodbye and Jan and I made our way back to the Sally Ann.

Jan was really keen on her boyfriend and talked about him all night in the room. She kept on and on about me going back with her to his flat. Reluctantly, I agreed, just to shut her up so I could get some sleep. I was kind of glad I did after being thrown out of the hostel in the morning, along with the rest of the single mums and old dears. I didn't realise how long a day could be when you're wandering the streets with with nothing to do and nowhere to go.

Jan knew Dundee like the back of her hand. She took me on a guided tour, through streets busy with shoppers and traffic. It reminded me so much of Aberdeen. We headed to the Hilltown, an area on the edge of the city centre, and then walked all the way up to the top of the Law Hill, the highest point for miles around. The city stretched out before us as we watched the steady progress of ships sailing in and out of the docks now far below. The road and rail bridges snaked across the River Tay to the Fife coast in the far distance. I wondered what it was like living there. It looked so pretty and inviting with the green fields all bathed in sunshine.

I caught Jan looking at her watch again. Then she nodded. It was time to go to her boyfriend's flat. So we made our way down the hill and headed towards Downfield, which was not too far away. I was glad to get there to rest my aching feet. Again I waited in the living room listening to another performance.

When they finished and came back through from the bedroom, Mick said he needed some air. He offered to walk us back to the hostel. I noticed he was very well dressed for someone who didn't work. His smart expensive Crombie wool coat hid a lean wiry frame. He didn't dress like most of the young men his age. His black hair was unfashionably short. He had high cheekbones and a thin, neatly trimmed moustache, and reminded me a little of the actor Clark Gable. Mick also had a strong Dundonian accent. He asked me if I liked staying at the Sally Ann. When I told him I didn't, he said he knew a lady who could put me up. She was on her own and would be glad of the company, someone to talk to. What did I think? He could take me up to see her tonight. She was a good friend of his and it wouldn't be a problem.

Jan butted in, rather annoyed. "Why are you helping her? I'm your girlfriend. You never help me," she said, in a raised voice.

They started arguing and I could only wonder why Mick wanted to help me and not her. Then he shouted she never was and never would be his girlfriend. She was nothing but a slut. I felt terrible, uncomfortable, embarrassed by the two of them, yet again. All I wanted to do was run away.

"You bastard!" she roared out, storming off down the road into the distance.

Mick watched her for a moment or two and then turned to me, saying, "Do you want to go and see my friend, or not?"

I couldn't believe his uncaring attitude. Jan no longer mattered. She was dumped without a thought. I wasn't sure whether to run after her or not. The argument completely unsettled me, reinforcing my initial instinct that Mick was someone to be wary of and not to be trusted. He was a user. But what could I do? The little money I had was dwindling fast. I still had no job to go to so I would be on the street again, very soon. So I agreed to go with him to see what his friend was like. What harm could it do? If I didn't like her, I didn't have to stay with her.

Mick's friend didn't stay that far away. She lived on the first floor of a run-down building which was converted into small flats. We climbed up a winding staircase and then knocked on a blue door. The lady who answered seemed to know Mick well. She invited us both inside. I waited in the living room while Mick spoke with her privately in the kitchen. She returned a few minutes later and introduced herself as Gladys, saying any friend of Mick's was a friend of hers. She would be happy to put me up. I could stay as long as I wanted and could come and go as I pleased.

Gladys was a small thin woman, aged somewhere in her middle forties, with long brown hair and thick-framed glasses. I noticed she wore a wedding ring. But there were no tell-tale signs of a husband anywhere to be seen in the flat. She had no airs or graces either. I picked up a hardness in her voice. There was also a hardness in the way she held herself. I knew life had been anything but kind.

Mick suddenly announced he had bits and pieces to do and so had to leave us. But before he left, he asked me if I would like to go out with him tomorrow night to see the sights of Dundee.

"What about Jan?" I said.

"What about her? We're finished. I'll be back here tomorrow for you, round about 7 o'clock."

He was out the door and away before I had a chance to think about it. Everything happened so quickly. I dreaded having to go to the hostel to pick up my belongings. Jan was bound to think I'd stolen Mick from her, but it wasn't true. I only needed somewhere to stay. But I was afraid she wouldn't see it like that. When I went to the hostel a couple of hours later, she was nowhere to be seen, so I quickly threw my belongings into my case and left feeling rather guilty. I never saw her again.

Mick called for me at the appointed time. As we walked around the city centre, he pointed out all the places of interest. I enjoyed myself and began to think I'd judged him a bit too harshly. After he walked me back to Gladys's flat, he asked if he could take me out again the following afternoon.

We went to Camperdown Park, Dundee's largest public park. As we strolled among the trees, Mick told me he'd liked me from the first moment he saw me. I was shy and didn't know what to say, never having had a boyfriend before. It was a new experience.

Later on in the week we walked to the top of the Law Hill and stood silently in the darkness, looking down over the city ablaze with thousands of lights. Mick moved closer to me, gently placing my hand in his before asking me to marry him. Although this was the most romantic of settings to propose to me, I was taken aback. I had no idea this was coming. There was only silence between us. He told me to think it over.

On the way back, Mick dropped another bombshell. Gladys's husband was in the jail for murder. He was a real hard man. Some guy crossed him so he went looking for him with an axe. He found him in a crowded pub and axed him to death in front of everyone.

"He's coming out of jail soon," warned Mick.

"Why didn't you tell me before?" I said, my voice rising in a panic.

"I didn't know he was getting out. I only just found out myself," Mick tried to explain.

"No way I'm staying there with an axe murderer. Sounds like a real nutter."

"Calm down," he said. "I'll sort something out."

No matter how hard Mick tried to reassure me, I didn't calm down. Gladys was a nice lady and we got on well, but I'd never be able to sleep in my bed at night knowing he was in the next room. "What am I going to do? Where am I going to live?" I shouted.

"I'll ask my gran. She'll put you up. Don't mention to Gladys I told you about her husband."

I said I wouldn't. Without realising it, I began to trust Mick. If he said he would sort things out, then things would be sorted out. The weight was lifted from my shoulders. There was no need to worry. I felt much calmer. No mention was made of his marriage proposal as he kissed me in front of Gladys's front door.

When we went inside, Mick asked Gladys if he could stay the night because it was so late. She said he could, but he'd have to sleep on the settee. I was a little surprised at that but happy enough because I still felt a bit unsettled after learning about Gladys's husband. With Mick there, everything would be fine.

I told Gladys I was leaving in the morning to stay with Mick's gran and I thanked her for putting up with me and helping me out. She said she was sorry to see me go and would miss my company. When I told her I'd pop back and see her whenever I could, she was much happier. After sorting Mick out with some blankets and a spare pillow, Gladys went to bed. I talked with Mick for a few minutes more and then went through to my bedroom to sleep.

Suddenly, I was aware of Mick standing over me in the darkness of the room, shaking me awake, telling me not to be frightened. I didn't know what was happening and just lay there in the bed, petrified, unable to move a muscle. He undressed himself and then climbed on top of me, pressing his body hard against mine. I couldn't move or do anything. He was too strong. It was all over in a couple of minutes. He said nothing as he left the room. I felt dirty and angry and used.

It was late in the morning when I awoke. I went through into the living room to find Mick was nowhere to be seen. Gladys had already put the blankets and pillow away and noticed how down I looked.

"What's wrong with you?" she finally asked. "I don't know what happened to Mick. He was gone when I got up this morning."

She asked me if I wanted some tomato soup and placed a bowl on the table for me, but I had no appetite. I stirred the contents around and around with my spoon, gazing into the bowl, saying nothing.

Gladys piped up, "What's the matter? Cheer up. Things can't be that bad!"

"They are," I said.

She looked at me with a concerned, kindly expresion and I blurted out everything.

"Were you a virgin, Pat?"

"Yes," I said.

She was furious. "What he did was wrong. He had no right to do what he did," she said.

The conversation was suddenly interrupted by Mick walking through the front door, smiling, acting as if nothing was wrong. But before he could take another step, I hurled the bowl at him, splattering his coat in tomato soup. He just stood there, rooted to the spot, with his mouth wide open and a stunned expression on his face.

"What have I done?"

"I hate you!" I cried out, with as much venom as I could muster.

He spoke softly, trying to calm me down. "Is it about last night?"

"Yes, you know it is," I said.

"She's every right to be upset. What you did was wrong," said Gladys. "But maybe it's best if I leave you two to sort it out."

With that, she got up from the table and went to her bedroom.

"Look Pat, I'm marrying you. I love you. I honestly didn't think you'd mind," said Mick, trying his hardest to apologise. "I'll never do that again without asking. I promise."

He kept on and on, saying sorry and begged me for another chance. I felt I had no option given the situation I was in. He was the only person looking out for me. I believed he really did love me, so I forgave him. He took me to his gran's place which turned out to be the same flat in Downfield where I first met him. I was under the mistaken impression it was his flat. Mick noticed the puzzled look on my face.

"It's my gran's flat. I live here with her," he explained. "And so does my grandad and uncle." Mick told me they were all normally out during the day. His uncle worked on the buses and his grandad in a factory. His gran was usually out visiting her buddies or at the bingo. Now I understood why Jan had been so conscious of the time whenever she came up for a visit. That was why they wasted no time in getting down to business.

I met Mick's gran when she returned home from the afternoon bingo session, complaining it was all a waste of money. She was a small woman with a sharp tongue and put me in mind of a tiny ant, always scurrying here, there and everywhere. At every opportunity, she lashed out at everyone and everything, threatening to take an overdose if she wasn't getting the attention from us she thought she deserved. Mick looked at me and chuckled at the horrified expression on my face. "Don't worry, she's always saying that. She never does. It's only for effect. You'll get used to her."

Mick's gran was a strange woman who could also be very kind at times. Often, she offered to do my washing for me. Every Sunday morning, she made us a Dundee special, a strange concoction of mince with baked beans mixed through it. It tasted delicious and was very filling. But whenever we could, we preferred to avoid her as much as possible. So we went out to the pub, or to the cinema, or to meet Mick's friends. The flat became more of a place to eat and sleep. We were happy together and didn't argue very much. I was still looking for a job but Mick told me not to worry about it. He always seemed to have enough money to pay his gran for our digs and to take me out every evening. I never questioned where he got the money to pay for it all.

One evening, after returning home from the cinema, Mick's uncle and gran and grandad were sitting up waiting for us. They looked rather serious. Mick's uncle was a tall thin man who was balding on top. He told us it was time we started to think about moving out and getting a flat of our own. The flat was too overcrowded with five people living in it. I saw his point. There wasn't much space in the living room. It was all but taken up with the double bed I slept in. He said he was always getting disturbed by us coming in late. Because he was changing his shifts to the early shift, he needed his sleep. Mick understood and told them he would try his best to get us somewhere else to live as quickly as possible.

Over the coming days, Mick scoured the newspapers. He kept asking his friends if they knew of anywhere and chased up lead after lead. Finally, he found a flat we could afford, in the Stobswell area of the city. The only problem was they wanted a deposit and a month's rent in advance before handing over the keys. Mick explained the situation to his uncle who hummed and hawed and finally agreed to lend us the money. The small ground-floor flat was the first place I could truly call my own home. It was reasonably furnished with a combined sitting room and kitchen and a bedroom. Every day I scrubbed and cleaned it, to keep the place spick and span. I was so proud of my new home.

Within days of moving in, Mick started disappearing for hours on end. He always left the flat smartly dressed, in a three-piece suit. I had no idea where he went. Whenever I asked him, his reply was always vague. He said he was meeting his friends. So I pottered about the flat looking for things to do, just to keep myself occupied.

One afternoon, he came back with one of his friends in tow. They both looked hot and sweaty and out of breath, as if they'd been running for miles. Mick seemed different, excited, animated. He told me to get ready because we were all going into town shopping to buy some new clothes. Then he turned to his friend and they began speaking to each other in a strange sort of language. I never heard him talking this way before and didn't know what to make of it. Later, I learned it was called eggy. They put the word egg before every vowel, hiding the meaning of the sentence. I hated it when he talked that way.

"By the way, this is Frankie, my best mate," said Mick, casually, realising we'd not been introduced.

Frankie was small and stocky, with short brown hair. He never spoke much to me as we all walked into town. I asked Mick where he got the money from. He said he backed a couple of horses at the bookies. Both of them were 100–1 outsiders, but they still won. I didn't know what he was talking about, never having been in a bookies in my life. He pulled out a wad of cash and held it in the air and kissed it. "We're rolling in it," he announced, with a big grin on his face.

There must have been hundreds of pounds in his hand. I never saw so much money in all my life. We descended on the shops wide eyed, like a bunch of excited school kids. Frankie still never said anything. I got the feeling he felt left out with Mick heaping all the attention on me. It felt fantastic, walking around the shops knowing I could buy whatever I wanted. But it soon became clear Mick had other ideas, for he began to pick dresses for me, holding them up for me to wear.

"Try this one on," he said, as if giving me an order.

So I found myself doing exactly as I was told, trying on the clothes which Mick chose for me. I didn't have a say in the matter. Whenever I tried to choose something I wanted, he said he didn't like it and wouldn't pay for it. He pulled some boots from a shelf and told me to put them on. They were really expensive, made of suede. When I zipped them up, they reached just above my knees. Mick slowly eyed me up and down several times. I felt uncomfortable.

"Right, we'll buy them," he said.

His behaviour angered me. It began to show. Although the clothes he picked for me were lovely, I wanted to choose something that I wanted, not what he wanted. He noticed how upset I was becoming. So he gave me some money and pulled Frankie over to the men's department, leaving me to look at some coats. I picked out a lightweight raincoat with a red silk hanky sewn into the pocket. It was a really smart looking coat. So I bought it. Mick came back after buying some shirts and was furious when I showed him the coat.

"That's for fucking skinhead girls. You're not wearing that!" he roared out.

I felt very hurt and embarrassed. Everyone in the busy store was now watching us intently. But there was nothing he could do because I had already paid for it. By the time we all got back to the flat, Mick had cooled off, although he still warned me I wasn't ever to wear the coat again.

Next day, he made an appointment for me at the hairdresser. Again I had no choice in the matter. He did it without telling me. I just had to drop everything and go. He even left the hairdresser instructions how my hair was to be cut and styled. Then he dragged me along to the dole where he claimed money for us both, but I never once saw a penny.

Mick disappeared more and more over the coming days and weeks. I still had no idea what he was up to. But I trusted him. Our relationship, for the most part, was tender and passionate. When we made love, beautiful shades of blue and pink flooded my mind, immersing me in some strange, mystical power over which I had no control. But there were other times I was left feeling dirty and vulnerable, when he ordered me to stand naked in front of him holding a lit candle.

"Turn towards the window," he shouted out.

I turned slowly in the semi-darkness, scared witless, playing out some weird scene he conjured up in his head. I felt his eyes lusting over my naked form in the soft glow of the candlelight. But I wasn't playing the part properly.

"Do it again. Walk slowly towards me. Hold the candle higher," he screamed.

I wanted desperately to grab a blanket to cover myself, to hide my vulnerability, to wrap it around me so I felt safe. But I didn't want to displease him either. His eyes feasted once more on my naked flesh until he felt aroused enough and I was sufficiently degraded. He enjoyed the power he had over me.

One afternoon, he said he had to see someone and asked me to go with him. He took me to a large office block in the centre of town. The person he was supposed to see was still busy with another client, so the receptionist told us to take a seat and wait. I still had no idea why we were there. I kept asking Mick but he never gave me a straightforward answer. He looked uncomfortable.

A middle-aged man finally appeared in front of us and Mick told me to sit and wait outside while he went in. This wouldn't take very long. The man obviously knew Mick and that I was his girlfriend, so he also invited me to join them. Mick wasn't happy at the idea but appeared to have no choice. Inside, the man introduced himself as Mick's probation officer. I had no idea what that meant. He asked Mick if he was keeping out of trouble. Mick said he was. Then he asked him if he had found a job yet.

"No," said Mick.

The probation officer, who was sitting behind his desk, turned slightly and looked at me. I was sitting directly in front of him, on the only chair available in the office. Mick was standing at the side of me.

"And what about your girlfriend. Does she know about you?"

Mick squirmed and shifted his weight from one leg to another.

"No. I haven't told her anything."

A Pandora's box opened up as the probation officer reeled off a list of past misdeeds and crimes stretching back many years. Now I knew it all: Mick's dark secrets, the mindless acts of vandalism when he was a young kid, the assaults, the drug dealing, the stretches inside. He'd hidden everything from me so well and now I didn't know him.

My gut instincts were right all along. He really was trouble. But by the time we arrived back at the flat, Mick convinced me he'd changed his life around. He was now on the straight and narrow and determined to make a better life for us both. And I believed him. After all, I convinced myself, I never once saw him doing anything wrong.

Up until that point, when Mick disappeared for hours it was always during the day. When he came back at night, we usually went out somewhere, often to the pub, or sometimes to the dancing or to see a film at the cinema. But then he started going out by himself at night, first picking an argument with me so he could storm off. He returned home drunk but was usually happy and chatty and full of apologies. But one night, there was something different about him. I couldn't put my finger on it. He looked preoccupied, broody, and wouldn't tell me what was wrong. There was no apology either.

"Who've you been screwing when I'm out?" he suddenly screamed out.

I was stunned, frightened, frozen to the spot. His faced was changed. He was suddenly transformed into a monster and I felt helpless. I didn't understand what was happening. I watched horrified as he ran through to the bedroom, peering under the bed as if looking for someone or for some evidence. Then he ran to the window.

"Where's the fucking cunt hiding?" He kept on and on, screaming out the same question. Then he grabbed me by the hair and pulled me around the room. I yelled out in pain.

"Where's he hiding?"

"Honestly, there's no one here," I cried out, begging him to stop. But he didn't believe me. "Lying bitch!" He smacked me hard across the face with the back of his hand. I stumbled and fell to the floor. Then he kicked me again and again. I curled up into a tight ball to protect myself. When the beating finally stopped, Mick walked over to the settee and lay down without another word and stared up at the ceiling.

How long I lay there, on the floor, feet away from him, terrified, I don't know. I watched his face through half-opened eyes, not daring to move an inch. Eventually, he fell asleep. I crawled across the floor to the bedroom and managed somehow to pull myself up onto the bed. I ached all over. The darkness felt comforting and safe. I tried to work out what had just taken place. Why had he acted this way, with such violence, when I had done nothing wrong? There were no answers. I sobbed my eyes out until I fell asleep.

Chapter Nineteen

THE COLD WATER felt soothing as I gently splashed my face. At first, I was too frightened to look in the bathroom mirror at my reflection. I knew I wouldn't recognise the 16-year-old girl staring back at me. She looked battered and bruised, a real mess, with red swollen lips and eyes. I turned away and pulled a comb through my hair and winced in pain. My scalp still hurt too much. I gave up.

Mick was in the kitchen when I went through, scrubbing hard at the cupboards, hardly able to look at me. He scrubbed so hard I got the feeling he was trying to do some kind of penance for what he did, attempting to wash away the stain, the memory of last night. I couldn't talk to him. I didn't want to. He knew what he did to me and he'd have to deal with it himself, without any words of comfort or forgiveness from me. I made myself a cup of tea and left him to get on with it. Later on, he tried to make amends by suggesting I go back to Aberdeen and visit my sister.

"It'll do you some good. You've not seen her in a while. You can spend some time with her. What do you think?"

"Yes," I replied, grudgingly. It would be nice, I thought to myself. I hadn't seen Lottie or the boys for a few months now and I missed her company, talking late into the night over many cups of tea. More than anything, I needed some space, to get away and to think whether my relationship with Mick was worth continuing. But I didn't want my sister to see my face like this. So I decided to wait until the swelling died down. Over the coming days, Mick couldn't have been nicer to me, saying sorry all the time and promising never to hit me again. Our relationship seemed better than ever.

Early one morning, he asked me to get ready. We were going out for the day with his friend Frankie. I asked him where to, but he was evasive, saying only I would see. We caught a bus across the Tay Bridge to a small picturesque village somewhere in Fife. I didn't know where we were as we strolled along quiet streets with old quaint cottages on either side. Brightly coloured flowers tumbled out of window boxes set against whitewashed walls. The smell of lavender hung in the air as we passed by neat and tidy gardens filled with lupins and roses.

We came to a small hotel and went around the side and up a narrow dimly lit staircase. Mick said he had to meet someone in one of the hotel rooms. So I followed him and Frankie without thinking much about it. I found myself in an empty room and Frankie stood outside as if on guard. Mick put a finger to his lips to tell me to be quiet before bending down and pulling out a large suitcase from under the bed. It was as if he knew it was already there, just waiting for him. I felt uncomfortable. Something didn't feel right.

Mick opened the suitcase and pulled out tight bundles of money, each one secured by an elastic band. He stuffed them into his suit pockets. After pushing the suitcase back under the bed, we hurriedly left the hotel the way we came in. My mind was filled with dark gloomy thoughts as we sat on the bus taking us back home. Mick and Frankie seemed on a high, talking eggy so I wouldn't understand them. What were they hiding from me? Mick promised me he was going straight. Now I felt I was being sucked into some kind of seedy shadowy world. He was up to no good. I felt helpless.

Not long afterwards, Mick took me to a pub I'd never been to before. It was dark and grubby. The atmosphere felt cold and unfriendly, nothing like the pubs we normally went to. I sat down. Mick walked up to the bar to get me a vodka and orange. Then he said he had some business to sort out, which wouldn't take very long. All about me, small groups of men huddled around tables, talking and arguing amongst themselves. Their voices rose and fell, then tailed off into whispers. I felt like a duck out of water. But I was also fascinated. Suddenly, there were handshakes all round, as if deals had been struck.

When Mick came back, we went downstairs to the basement where some man with a larger than life personality was talking to everyone. The man wore a white suit with a bright red carnation through the buttonhole. Mick introduced me as his girlfriend. Then he wished him a happy birthday. There was something dark and menacing about the man as I shook his hand. He smiled, showing a mouthful of gold fillings. Mick appeared nervous and edgy. I never saw him act this way before. He made some excuse about finding a seat, but I knew it was just to get away from this man. I didn't like the people or the pub and just wanted to go home.

But Mick warned me the man in the white suit would take great offence if we just walked out and left. He wasn't the sort of person to cross. I wasn't sure what Mick meant by that. But later, when everyone was up dancing, we managed to slip away quietly, without anyone noticing. When I asked Mick who he was, he said it was best I didn't ask any more questions.

ᘒᑊᕬ

By now, the swelling on my face had died down enough so I could go and visit my sister. I kissed Mick goodbye at the bus station and told him not to worry and that I'd see him again in a week. I was very glad to see Lottie and to catch up with all her news. If she noticed anything wrong with my face, she never mentioned it.

As I walked along the familiar streets of the city centre, looking at all the shops, I bumped into Doreen, whom I last met at the YWCA hostel. I told her I was pleased to see her and I bore her no grudges for involving me in the chequebook incident with Cathy. But there was something different about her. She'd lost her spark. I asked her if she was feeling all right.

"I'm OK", she answered, sounding hesitant and depressed.

"Where are you working?" I said, trying hard to keep the conversation going.

Her eyes turned away and looked at the ground. She spoke almost in a whisper. "I'm a prostitute," she said.

Hardly believing what I heard, I said, "Oh Doreen, that's awful. You can't do that! What made you do it?"

"Money. Can't live on fresh air."

"But there must be something else you can do?"

"Well, there isn't!"

She was getting annoyed at me, thinking I was condemning her. But I wasn't. I was just really surprised and saddened. Then I told her about my flat in Dundee and about Mick.

"Why don't you come back with me? I'll help you until you find a decent job and get a place of your own."

She was taken aback by the suggestion. I saw she was thinking hard about it and I wanted to reassure her.

"You've nothing to lose. Go on, give it a try," I said, hoping to persuade her.

She shrugged her shoulders and answered, "I'll see."

I told her to think it over. I was catching the bus to Dundee on

Friday night and would look out for her. With that, she turned and walked away, disappearing a few seconds later among the crowds of shoppers.

Friday arrived all too quickly. I hated saying goodbye. It was so hard. I'd miss my sister and the boys. But I was excited at the prospect of seeing Mick again. I was also wondering if Doreen would turn up at the bus station.

"Hello Pat!"

I turned around sharply. It was Doreen. She had been to the hairdresser and now looked all pretty with her hair cut and styled. What a transformation as she stood in front of me, wearing a white raincoat and carrying a small brown bag. She was so much brighter now and talked enthusiastically about starting a new job and getting on with her life. When we got back to the flat, Mick was happy to see me. But there was a puzzled look on his face as he held the front door open.

"This is a friend from Aberdeen," I explained, introducing Doreen. "She's nowhere to live so I said she could stay with us, if that's all right? Just until she gets herself sorted."

I didn't tell Mick anything about Doreen's past or he would have thrown her out into the street. Doreen said she didn't mind sleeping on the settee as I handed her a pillow and a couple of spare blankets. After we all had something to eat, I said goodnight and Mick and I went through to our bedroom. I was exhausted and quickly fell asleep.

In the early hours of the morning, I suddenly awoke for no good reason, expecting Mick to be lying next to me. Still half asleep, I lifted my head from the pillow, looking around the bedroom. But there was no sign of him. So I got out of bed to check where he was. I switched on the light and opened the bedroom door and gasped. The light from the bedroom flooded across the living room floor, illuminating two naked bodies locked together. Mick turned his head, startled, transfixed, and leapt off. I flew at him.

I screamed, "How could you!"

"She led me on," he squirmed, trying to push the blame away.

Doreen sat up and grabbed a blanket and quickly wrapped it around herself. She said nothing, offering up no defence, and just stared at the floor to avoid looking me in the eye.

"Pack your bags and get out. We're finished. No more excuses!"

Mick knew I meant it. It was the first time he saw such a rage in me. I never knew such fury existed inside me either. He fumbled at his shirt buttons and pulled up his trousers. Then he beat a hasty retreat out the door, mumbling something about picking up the rest of his clothes in the morning. I was glad to see the back of him. Doreen sat dumbly on the settee, still clutching the blanket.

"I suppose you want me to leave, too?"

"No, Doreen. It's him I don't trust," I replied with a heavy sigh. "If it wasn't you, it would be someone else."

I explained my relationship with Mick was not the kind I wanted. I was never enough for him. After calming down, I told Doreen we would have to get jobs because Mick paid the rent for the flat and bought all the food.

"Look, Pat, what I did was wrong. I don't know why it happened. He just came through and that was it."

I cut Doreen off. "I don't want to hear any more. What's done is done. That's it, finished."

We never spoke about it again. The following morning, Doreen didn't seem worried about the dire situation we were now in. She seemed confident of finding a job. I couldn't face seeing anyone because I still felt too angry and hurt inside. So I sat about the flat, moping, waiting for Doreen to return, replaying all the events of the last few days and weeks in my head. I still wasn't sure whether I'd acted in haste throwing Mick out.

The day passed and Mick hadn't yet picked up his clothes. The key turned in the front door and Doreen walked through carrying bags of shopping. She sounded excited, telling me she managed to get a job in a small shop. The shop was desperate for someone, so she got started right away. She also convinced the boss to give her a sub out of her wages to buy some food.

I was over the moon knowing we would have something to eat. Doreen left each day to go to work and brought back some food each night. Then she started coming home later and later. Sometimes it was 9 o'clock before she appeared. I started to become suspicious. She was keeping some very odd hours for working in a shop. So I asked her where she worked. But she never answered me, always changing the subject.

One night, I asked her straight out. "Are you working as a prostitute?"

There was no answer.

"I'm not stupid. You're not working in a shop, are you? Just tell me the truth," I demanded.

"No. I'm getting paid sleeping with an old man. He lives just up the road."

I was angry again. The thought of Doreen using her body to buy us food turned my stomach. It wasn't right and I realised she'd no intentions of changing her life. My efforts to help her were in vain. All she was interested in was easy money and I couldn't have that on my conscience.

"I think it's best if you leave, Doreen. It's not going to work out."

She didn't look too happy. "No worries," she snapped back. "Just as well I've got somewhere to go."

She packed her belongings and stormed off in a huff, leaving me feeling very sad. I wanted so much for things to work out because she told me at the YWCA how she hadn't had it easy. Her mum died and her dad, a policeman, remarried. There were fierce arguments with her stepmum who kicked her out of the house when she was 16. Doreen slipped into prostitution without realising it. It wasn't something she planned.

Now with Doreen and Mick both gone, the silence in the flat was deafening. The worries felt overwhelming. How was I going to pay the rent? There was hardly any food left in the cupboards. I would have to find some kind of job very quickly and it still probably wouldn't cover everything. As I sat worrying, trying to work things out, there was a sharp knock on the door. I opened it and Mick barged through, knocking me clean off my feet and into the wall. He demanded the clothes back he bought me and stormed through to the bedroom, frantically opening the chest of drawers I kept them in.

"I bought that!" he shouted, holding up a blouse. Then he ripped it down the middle and threw it to the floor.

"Get out!" I yelled back. "I'm going to call the police."

"Call the fucking police. Think I care?"

Holding up my skirts, he tore them to shreds, one by one. He was like a mad demented animal. Everything he ever bought me, he said, he was going to destroy. When he was satisfied there was nothing left, he went over to the mirror above the fireplace and took the photographs of us in happier times and ripped them up. The tiny pieces lay scattered all around the living room carpet. He surveyed the flat for a moment or two, pleased by his handiwork, and then brushed me aside.

"Who wants to live with a cow like you anyway?" he sneered, before slamming the front door behind him.

The bedroom looked like the aftermath of a battle. Ripped-up clothes lay scattered between the upturned drawers which were lying at odd angles. I broke down and wept. Could my life get any worse? I knew I had to get myself out of this mess. Checking my purse, I counted out the little money I had and figured it was enough to pay for my bus fare into town to the employment exchange. Tomorrow, I would have to get myself some kind of a job.

❀

The bus drew slowly up to the bus stop. As I got up from my seat to get off I felt my coat being grabbed from behind. Before I could react, I heard a loud tearing sound and caught a fleeting glimpse of Mick dashing past. He jumped off the bus and ran into the distance. The only coat I possessed was now in tatters.

I had no idea he had followed me on to the bus, waiting for this opportunity to strike. The passengers stared at me in disbelief. Some old dears asked me if I was all right, saying how shocking it all was. It was pointless now going to the employment exchange. I wouldn't make the right impression with my coat hanging off my back.

Mick's antics were starting to really upset me now as I made my way home to the flat. All the clothes I had in the world were the ones I was wearing. My situation was now so desperate I started stealing packets of soup from the local corner shop. It was the only way I could feed myself. I'm sure the lady behind the counter suspected something, but for some strange reason, she never let on. Two or three times a week I walked out the shop hiding the packets of soup under my jumper, never actually buying anything.

Bella, my next door neighbour, invited me in to her flat one evening, telling me how sorry she was things hadn't worked out between Mick and me, but I was better off without him. She said I could do much better than living with someone with such violence in him. I knew she was right. She made me a cup of tea and offered me a fresh baked roll her brother had just collected from the all-night bakery up the road. It felt so good having something more than just soup to eat.

I liked Bella a lot. She had a warm Irish accent and took great pride in her personal appearance. I knew she didn't have much in the way of money. Most of her time was taken up with looking after her brother who had mental problems. She felt sorry for me having so few clothes to wear because of Mick and his carry on and asked if I wanted a pair of blue trousers she no longer wore. I gratefully accepted her kind offer and went next door to my flat and tried them on. They were a perfect fit.

There was a knock at the door and I was surprised to see Doreen standing there. It was just a short visit, she said. She was now living with a divorced man many years older than herself. He worked as a brickie and was very good to her.

"I've got a real sugar daddy," she winked.

I couldn't help smiling back. Doreen could never resist the lure of money. "He'd better have plenty of money then, to keep you going."

"Don't worry. I made sure of that before I moved in with him," she laughed.

"Good luck with him. Hope it all works out for you. Knowing you, I'm sure it will."

I was about to make Doreen another cup of tea when there was a knock on the door again. Who else could it be? I wondered, because I didn't exactly have many friends. As I pulled the door back, my whole body froze. It was Mick, screaming something about the trousers I was wearing.

"Who have you been whoring it with?" he roared out, his face contorted in rage.

Everything went into slow motion. I remember the cold menacing look in his eyes and lying out in the damp dark street, fending off kicks and punches, hearing screams from Doreen and Bella from somewhere far away in the distance. Then everything went black. I woke up in hospital. There was hardly a part of my body that didn't hurt. Miraculously, the X-rays showed nothing was broken. My injuries were superficial. A few hours later, I was discharged and sitting back in my flat.

The landlord paid me a visit the following morning with an ultimatum: pay the rent or get out at the end of the week. Although he found it difficult looking at my bruised and battered face, there was no pity in his voice as he turned and walked out the door. Who was going to employ me looking like this? I thought. My situation was hopeless. I had no job, no clothes, no food and now it looked like I'd have nowhere to stay in a few days' time. The heels on my one and only pair of shoes were so run down I felt like a tramp.

The police turned up later that day, asking me if I wanted to press charges. It was difficult to talk because my jaw and lip hurt so much, but I managed to whisper yes. I knew the police would find Mick now and lift him. It wasn't a day too soon as far as I was concerned. He had just about destroyed my confidence, leaving me feeling like a little frightened mouse, scared to go out the door in case I bumped into him.

A couple of days later, the police returned. They told me Mick had been charged and bailed and warned not to come anywhere near me or he would be lifted again. So I felt it was safe enough to visit Doreen. She lived only a short distance away. When she opened the door, she let out a gasp, hardly able to believe the mess my face was in. We talked about the events of that night. I could see she felt really bad she wasn't able to do more for me.

"You did well, Doreen. No one could have stopped him," I reassured her. "He was possessed, crazy."

Doreen led me through to the living room, telling me to make myself at home. Her sugar daddy was nowhere to be seen. I explained my predicament and asked her for help. "I can't even afford a pair of new shoes," I moaned. "Look at the state of them."

"Yes, you do need new shoes." Doreen said if it was down to her, she would have no problem putting me up. But her fancy man would never warm to the idea. She had a thought, though. He was always too tired to clean up the flat.

"The kitchen is an absolute mess, and you know me, I hate cleaning. I can't get into housework. I'm sure he would give you money for a new pair of shoes if you cleaned up the kitchen. He's always complaining about it."

Doreen promised to try to sort something out and would call around in a couple of days' time to let me know one way or the other. So I left her flat feeling a little happier and a lot more hopeful. I didn't expect her to turn up the next morning.

"Does that mean I've got the job?"

"If you still want it," she said.

"And he'll pay me?"

"Of course he will! Do you want to start now?"

We went back to her flat. Doreen told me to take a deep breath. The kitchen was a real mess and hadn't been touched in days. Piles of plates covered in greasy fat lay everywhere in lopsided stacks. They were welded together by the remnants of brown and red sauce. After wading through them and wiping the cupboards and bunkers down and scrubbing the floor, it had the feel of a brand new kitchen. I called Doreen through. Her face lit up as she admired my hard work.

"He'll be really pleased," she said. "If you come back tomorrow evening, there'll be a new pair of shoes waiting for you."

I can't say I was too happy at that. I was expecting the money in my hand and now her fancy man was buying the shoes for me. But I didn't want to seem ungrateful. Beggars couldn't be choosers. When I came back the following day to collect them, he was waiting for me, standing next to a plain black pair of flat shoes neatly placed beside him on the carpet. He smiled.

"I've got the shoes," he said, pausing. "How bad do you want them? You know, you're a really pretty girl."

I felt uncomfortable, puzzled, as he eyed me slowly up and down. Doreen let out a smirk, enjoying my discomfort.

"I've cleaned the kitchen. They're my shoes now."

He picked the shoes up and dangled them in front of me. "How bad do you want them?" he repeated once more.

I realised he had other ideas, obviously knowing how desperate my situation was. I almost knew what was coming next.

"If you let me have sex with you, I'll let you have the new shoes."

"No way I'm sleeping with you. What do you think I am?" I shouted. "We had an agreement." He was gross, repulsive, dirty, old enough to be my father. A big fat stomach hung over his trousers. His shirt was covered in stains. Doreen laughed. I leapt forward, snatching the shoes from his hands and bolted out the door before he could react. You're not having me, I thought to myself.

I wasn't proud of what I did but the shoes were promised to me. I worked hard for them. When I got back to the flat, I tried them on and the heel flipped up and down walking across the carpet. The shoes were far too big. Never mind, I thought. Anything was better than wearing my old shoes. I stuffed them with newspaper to stop the heels slipping out and went to the shop to steal a packet of soup. I was starving. But I was stopped by a police car moments after stepping out the door. Doreen and her fancy man had reported me for stealing the shoes.

Sitting in the car, I tried to explain to the policeman how I worked hard for the shoes. They were mine. But he asked me to produce a receipt to prove it. Of course, I couldn't. I think he felt sorry for me, realising the state I was in. He said he wouldn't take the matter further provided I gave them back. He drove me over to Doreen's flat and I grudgingly handed them over without saying a word. What else could I do? The policeman was satisfied and let me off with a warning. He also advised me to go and see a social worker to get some help.

I walked back to the flat in my bare feet feeling like the whole world was against me, cursing Doreen and her fancy man with every breath. I pushed the key in the lock as usual. But it wouldn't turn, no matter how hard I tried. The lock was changed. In a panic, I flew around to the back of the flat to discover my old run-down shoes standing next to my brown suitcase. The landlord had thrown me out.

Chapter Twenty

SUMMER COLOURS were turning to autumn shades. My grubby jumper badly needed a wash. It was all I had to stop me from freezing to death in the cold winds which were beginning to bite. As I sat and waited to see a social worker, I didn't need to paint a picture. One look at me told the whole story. Tom, a young social worker, introduced himself. He said he had good Christian neighbours who lived downstairs from him.

"They're really nice people. I'm sure they'll help you out," he said. He spoke softly, with a well-defined English accent. Under different circumstances, I would have steered well clear of him. But I kept thinking about what the policeman said. The policeman told me to go and see a social worker. The words kept turning around in my mind and I was at rock bottom. There was no one else to turn to.

"Thank you," I replied, trying hard to fight back the tears.

If he had shown me any more kindness, I'm sure I would have broken down. I wasn't used to such compassion. He took me to a run-down housing estate filled with drab and squalid tenements. I was surprised a professional like Tom lived there amid the broken boarded-up windows and dark dingy closes strewn with rubbish. He told me it was all he could afford at the moment because he had just qualified. It didn't seem fair.

Tom was right about his neighbours. Jackie was from South Africa. Although living in such a poor area, she struck me as someone who came from a very privileged background. Slightly plump with short black hair, Jackie spoke well and seemed highly educated and appeared very comfortable with who she was. Her friend Helen was also well educated and didn't have the strong deep South African accent Jackie had. She was tall and slim and her platinum blonde hair hung down to her shoulders.

They said they were pleased to put me up. But I would have to share a room with Jackie. I felt relaxed and happy chatting away to them. They told me they were missionaries and planned to stay in Dundee for a year. Jackie suggested I should work as a community service volunteer. It didn't pay a lot, no more than pocket money, but accommodation and food were provided. She had some contacts who would get the ball rolling.

Jackie was passionate about cooking. At mealtimes, there was always a different South African delicacy ready on the table, waiting for us to enjoy. The aroma was mouth watering. They took it in turns to say grace and then we tucked in. Religion was never a talking point at the table, although they could easily have rammed God down my throat. But they didn't.

There was no radio or television in the flat, which felt cold and damp. Tom popped by on his way to work one morning and offered me some of his cast-off jumpers which I gratefully accepted. I promised to give them back once I had a job and could buy my own. Jackie and Helen held meetings most days in the flat with their missionary friends, so I usually made myself scarce. I went out for long walks or visited a young single mum living across the road. She was struggling to bring up her toddler son on very little money and had no one to talk to. While walking through the Hilltown, suddenly I saw Frankie, Mick's friend, heading towards me. I didn't know which way to run to get away.

But before I could do anything, he was standing in front of me with a mean look on his face, his voice low and threatening.

"Don't turn up to court."

I was lost for words. He pointed a finger to within an inch of my face.

"We know where you live. Turn up to court and we'll kick you in, maybe worse." He walked away then turned and shouted, "Remember, we're watching!"

I knew this was all Mick's doing and Frankie was just the messenger. But he succeeded in scaring me. There was no way I was turning up at the court. Not now. It wasn't worth it. I felt uneasy the rest of the day, edgy, always looking over my shoulder. How did he know where I lived?

That night I couldn't sleep. Frankie's threats kept playing over and over in my head until Jackie's voice broke through. "Can you see the light?"

"What light?" I said, peering in the darkness of the bedroom. I couldn't see a thing. What was she talking about? "No," I said.

The next night, just as I was dozing off, she asked me again, "Can you see the light?"

What was she going on about? I stared hard into the darkness to see if I could see this light she was getting all excited about. There was nothing but darkness. "No, I can't" I replied.

For a third night in a row, she asked me the same stupid question. I was beginning to think she wasn't right in the head, some kind of religious nut. She was never going to let it drop. Instead of saying no, I decided to play along. "Yes, yes, I can see the light. It's over there!" I exclaimed.

Jackie's voice boomed out and I nearly jumped out of my skin. "Hallelujah! Hallelujah! Praise the Lord. She sees the light!" Now satisfied her prayers were answered and my soul was saved, she went back to sleep. Thankfully, she never disturbed me again.

ঞ৯

The court case came and went but I knew nothing about it or any outcome. I made my way to Liff Hospital to start a job as a live in community service volunteer which Jackie managed to get me. I was shown around by the middle-aged doctor in charge.

When we entered ward 13, I was stunned. I could hardly bring myself to look. In front of me were rows of cots with tiny babies in them, all with huge swollen heads. My heart reached out to them. It was so sad. A little teddy lay next to each baby. The doctor said no one came to see them. Mother Nature was so cruel, I thought. The babies were unwanted, rejects, hidden away out of sight.

In the next ward were lots of happy young adults with Down's syndrome. They all gravitated towards us as soon as the doctor opened the door. A young girl grabbed my arm and led me over to a table where they were painting. She pushed a small paintbrush into my hand. They crowded around me, urging me to join in with them. The doctor was taken aback. He'd never seen them interact like this with anyone and watched amazed as we all painted together.

Later, he said he had a special job for me. The job meant I would have a small office with a telephone. I had to encourage patients to draw small triangles, circles and squares on a piece of paper. Then I had to write a report out on how each managed the task and send it upstairs to his office. It was a good job which I enjoyed very much. Some of the patients could be violent, so there was always a male nurse on hand when they came into my office. Normally, they wore a padded leather helmet to stop them hurting themselves and others around them.

I worked alongside a young social worker whose constant moaning started to get on my nerves. The social worker complained at every opportunity that he should have been given the job and the office, not me, because he was better qualified. He nagged and fussed like an old mother hen, and even warned me not go on dates with junior doctors. They were only after one thing. He was hard to ignore. It was difficult to believe he was even a professional because of his personal appearance, which he made no effort with. His hair was unkempt and hung halfway down his back. He always wore the same scruffy jeans and jacket. Maybe that was why the doctor never gave him the job.

I never went out on any dates with the junior doctors even though they often asked me. They all appeared to come from very posh backgrounds, so I felt I had nothing in common with them. But whenever I got the chance, I borrowed some of their medical textbooks which I took to my room and read for hours on end. I think they were all amazed at my interest in medicine. Some of the doctors even suggested I should think about medical school. But I knew that could never happen because of my lack of education.

For the first time in a very long time, I felt happy and settled, really enjoying the job, the room, and making lots of new friends. After work was finished for the day, my time was my own. I enjoyed going to the hospital discos in the evening and dancing with residents to the latest pop tunes.

Early one evening, while I was tidying up my room, there was an unexpected knock on the door. I was greeted by two policemen who said they had a warrant for my arrest. Not again, I thought, as I felt the colour draining from my face. They slapped a pair of handcuffs on me and led me down the main staircase of the hospital to the busy front entrance. I felt too ashamed and embarrassed to look anyone in the eye as the policemen ushered me into a waiting car. Before I knew it, I was sitting in a cell at the sheriff court, listening to the sound of the door slamming shut and the key turning in the lock. The police told me I was to appear in front of the sheriff in the morning, to explain why I hadn't turned up at court as a witness. I never mentioned I was too afraid to give evidence because Mick's friends would have kicked me in. Mick scared me more than any court appearance.

Early next morning, I was led out the cell to a holding area where I was surprised to see Doreen sitting on a bench, flanked by a policeman. She never once looked in my direction or acknowledged me in any way and just stared at the floor. I sat down on a separate bench, unaware at first that Mick was sitting out of sight around the corner. He heard me talking to the policeman guarding me and started shouting out how much he loved me. I heard the policeman in charge of him getting annoyed and telling him to shut up. It was only then I realised we must all have been arrested at the same time.

I was taken upstairs to the courtroom. It was empty except for the sheriff sitting on his bench, trying to appear stern and intimidating. No one explained what was expected of me as I stood in the dock. I almost burst out laughing at the sight of the sheriff's wig. If I'd taken the situation a bit more seriously, I wouldn't have argued with him either, or made up such a feeble excuse about missing the bus from Aberdeen. What a mistake. The sheriff saw right through the lie. He threw me right back downstairs again and into the same cell, where I spent the longest three days of my life.

All I had for company was two thick books. I attempted to read them, just to stop being driven up the walls with boredom. Jackie and Helen came to visit me, which was a welcome relief. But it was hard to keep the conversation going through the small bars in the cell door. I was dying for a fag. "Do you think you can get me some?" I pleaded, in desperation.

The pious, pitying look on their faces turned to one of disgust. They reminded me they were Christians. "Smoking is evil," said Jackie, almost without thinking.

Helen nodded in agreement. I went without a fag for the three days.

I never did understand what the books were all about. I was just thankful to leave them behind me and to step into the courtroom again, for the trial. This time, there was no arguing with the sheriff. Mick was already there, dressed in a smart suit and tie. He chose to represent himself and displayed an air of self righteous arrogance which impressed no one, least of all the sheriff.

Nobody was fooled by the barrage of questions either, fired first at Doreen and then at me, as he tried to twist our evidence around to make it appear he was the innocent victim. The sheriff saw right through his antics. At the end of the short trial, he sentenced Mick to three months in prison for assault. Then the sheriff turned and looked at me and said he never wanted to see me back in his court again. If I had any sense, I would go back home to Aberdeen.

The sheriff's word were still ringing in my ears as I stood outside the courtroom, glad to see daylight and to breathe in some fresh clean air. It was four days since my arrest at the hospital. So I was desperate to resume my job and to get my life back on track. But when I got to my room, I found a hastily scribbled note which had been slipped under the door. It was from the sister in charge of the ward and sounded urgent. She wanted me to report to her office immediately, so I wasted no time going there. I nervously knocked on the door and waited. A second or two later, a high-pitched voice asked me to enter.

The sister stood at the side of a large desk, her heavy frame leaning up against it for support. She said nothing at first then glanced at me up and down. It was obvious she was cross at having to deal with some minion far down the pecking order.

"Well," she said, pausing. "What do you have to say for yourself?" She didn't wait for an answer but cut me off as soon as I opened my mouth. "We don't tolerate such behaviour at this hospital."

"But ... but ..." I stammered, trying hard to get the words out.

Her voice got louder and louder and drowned out my words of explanation. It was obvious she didn't want to hear them.

"No, we would much prefer it if you left," she said, shaking her head from side to side, convincing herself it was best for everyone concerned. She told me to pack my bags and to leave the hospital immediately. I knew it was pointless trying to explain I would have nowhere to stay. She didn't want to hear anything I had to say.

I walked slowly out the hospital gates carrying my brown suitcase, unsure of what to do now or in what direction to go. My mind was numb. There was a sick feeling in the pit of my stomach.

I walked aimlessly for hours on end, through bustling busy streets, trying hard to think of a plan and envious of all the people passing by who seemed so sure of the direction they were going in. Evening was approaching fast and I knew I had to find somewhere to stay for the night. By now I was exhausted and hungry with only enough money on me to pay for a room at some cheap hostel somewhere. My attention was suddenly drawn to a man standing alone outside the front door of a bingo hall enjoying a cigarette.

I shouted across the road to him asking if he knew any cheap hostels in the area. Cupping a hand to an ear to indicate he couldn't hear me, he waved me across the road. He was small and stocky, aged about 50 with receding hair and wearing a white raincoat. I saw him glance at my suitcase.

"What's a lovely young lady like you doing wandering about with a suitcase?" he asked.

"I'm trying to find a hostel," I explained. "Somewhere not too expensive."

He turned his head up to the sky and paused for a moment then shook his head. "Sorry, I can't think of any around here." His eyes caught mine and I smelled a whiff of alcohol on his breath. "Are you homeless?"

"Yes," I said. "I really need to find somewhere quite quickly."

"You look like you're carrying the whole world on your shoulders."

I attempted a half-hearted smile. He told me his name was John. All his kids were grown up now, so there was plenty of room in his house. He could take me up to see his wife, if I wanted. She would be more than happy to help me out. "Can't have you wandering about with nowhere to live," he said.

John seemed genuine and kind. He was going to do his best to help me out, he said. I felt a huge sense of relief walking up the road next to him. But he had to call in at his friend's place first, just for a minute. Did I mind? I said I didn't. We climbed up the stairs of an old tenement block and then he walked into a flat without knocking. There were two men sitting on easy chairs next to an unlit fireplace. John told me to make myself comfortable next to him on the settee.

One of the two men was a taxi driver who talked about the huge tip he got from one of his passengers. He seemed uneasy, on edge. I got the distinct impression he was unhappy with John being there. He almost seemed afraid. The man sitting opposite him looked ill. He had black hair with wisps of grey showing through and was very thin. His complexion was white and pasty. He wore an old-fashioned heavy green coat to keep out the cold and dampness in the flat.

John asked him for a drink. The man got up slowly and went over to a sideboard where he reached in and pulled out a half bottle of whisky. Then he picked up a tumbler from on top of the sideboard and poured out a drink and handed it to John. I asked John when we were leaving to go up to his house to see his wife.

"In a minute," he snapped.

He raised the small glass to his mouth and downed the whisky in one gulp. The taxi driver and the ill man watched him intently with serious looks on their faces and exchanged fleeting glances. Just then John got up, saying he was going to the toilet, and left the room.

The taxi driver turned to me, and in a very low, worried-sounding voice whispered, "What are you doing with him? Don't you understand? You could be in danger."

"What do you mean?" I said.

"He's a murderer. He's not long out the jail for killing a young girl about your age."

Oh my God, I thought, I've got to get out of here. A hush fell on the room as John returned from the toilet and sat down next to me. I felt terrified and stood up and walked to the living room door, making an excuse to leave.

"No, no, wait," said John. "I said I'm taking you back to my wife. She'll look after you."

"Let the lassie go if she wants to," said the taxi driver.

John got up and tried to grab hold of me but the taxi driver jumped in quickly.

"Leave her alone!" he shouted.

John's face changed instantly. A fierce argument broke out which quickly turned into a fight. Suddenly, he produced a knife.

"Run! Run!" screamed the taxi driver.

As John lunged out wildly, stabbing the knife furiously into empty air, the taxi driver desperately held on to his coat to stop him getting to me. I bolted out the living room and into the hallway and dashed through the nearest door. By luck, it had a lock and key in it. I grabbed the key with shaking hands and turned it. The lock snapped shut. I backed away inch by inch from the locked door until the wall behind stopped me going any further. I began to pray.

But John wasn't finished with me yet. Somehow, he managed to force his way past the taxi driver. Now he was standing outside the room, screaming and spewing out filth and obscenities and stabbing at the door. The door buckled and shuddered and almost came off its hinges as he tried to burst it open. All the time, the taxi driver was trying to stop him. I heard the sounds of fists hitting flesh and bone and the crash of bodies banging against the door. I was powerless to do anything as I struggled for breath and my heart thumped madly in my chest. No, no, don't let him come through the door, I begged God, the saints and everything that was holy.

Then everything fell silent and I knew the struggle outside the door was over. But was John still lurking in the hallway, waiting for me to open the door? After what seemed like an eternity, I heard the taxi driver's voice.

"It's OK. I've got that madman out the house."

I was still too scared to open the door. The taxi driver persisted. In a gentle reassuring tone, he repeated over and over, "He's gone now. He's gone. You're OK now."

There was barely enough strength left in me to turn the key and open the door. I was really happy to see the taxi driver who poured me a drink in the living room to calm my nerves. His arms were covered in deep scratches and smears of blood criss-crossed his face. I knew how lucky I'd been. The taxi driver saved my life and it was only by the grace of God he was there at all. Someone was surely watching over me.

The ill man sat silently in his chair with a shocked expression on his face. It was all too much for him. I finished the drink and told the taxi driver I needed to get away as far as I could. He asked me if I had anywhere to stay and I said I was going to find a cheap hostel.

"You'll be lucky at this time of night," he pointed out. "Anyway, half these places are full of drunks. You don't want to go there. It's not safe."

So he suggested someone he knew might be able to put me up

for the night. Her name was May. He offered to run me over to her place in his taxi. I had nowhere to go and since she was a female, I felt I would be safe enough. The one-bedroom flat turned out to be clean and comfortable and May, a single mum with a little boy, struck me immediately as kind and down to earth. She said she was sorry for only being able to offer me the settee. But I was grateful for it.

May told me she was a prostitute and was expecting two clients shortly. I sat reading magazines on the settee while her son coloured in colouring books on the floor. He was a quiet contented little soul. The doorbell rang and May invited her clients into the hallway. I heard them haggling over the price. Two young Chinese men walked through with her to the bedroom. A short while later, there was an argument. May was refusing to have sex with them unless they wore a condom. They didn't seem happy about that.

"Take it or leave it," I heard her say.

She gave them no choice in the matter. I picked up a magazine again and started reading but was interrupted when one of the Chinese men came through to the living room. He complained bitterly he was being treated unfairly. When I told him it had nothing to do with me, he sat down quietly on a chair and waited for his friend. May appeared soon after and the two clients left.

"You can make really good money at this game," said May, holding a hot cup of tea in her hand.

"Yes, I'm sure you can," I replied, suspicious of where the conversation was now going.

"You'd have a home here. You're young. Someone like you could do really well," she added.

I told her I could never bring myself to do anything like that. May looked disappointed. She became annoyed. "Then you can't stay here. You have to earn your keep."

She didn't seem to realise I had no intentions of staying anyway. I was going in the morning, first thing. As I was getting ready to sleep on the settee, I realised my suitcase was still in the flat where I had my lucky escape. I dreaded the prospect of going back there, but I had no choice. It contained all I had in the world.

When I knocked on the door in the morning, I was surprised to hear the sounds of children laughing and shouting coming from inside the flat. A young boy with blond hair opened the door. He called through to his dad that there was somebody to see him. The ill man appeared and looked a little taken aback to see me again so soon. I explained about leaving the case behind and he invited me inside. The children were running wild in the bedrooms so he shouted at them to stop making a racket.

I felt agitated the moment I sat down on the easy chair. A strange feeling came over me and as he spoke, his words began to fade and trail off into the distance. A picture, a vision in full colour, suddenly filled my mind, pulling me in. In front of me stood a young slim woman poised at the edge of a loch. No one will miss me, she cried out, over and over again, staring into the deep dark water. I felt powerless to help her, transfixed, unable to move as she threw herself in and disappeared beneath the murky depths. Suddenly, the vision was gone and I was back in the living room once more.

"Have you heard anything I've said?" said the ill man, looking at me a little perplexed.

I couldn't answer him. My mind was still full of the raw emotions from the young woman. They were etched into my soul, making me want to run to the nearest loch myself and jump in. It was taking every ounce of willpower I possessed to resist the urge. My thoughts and her thoughts had somehow become locked together and I was battling to free myself.

It was then I realised the woman in the vision was the wife of the ill man. She had lost all reason and killed herself and left her husband to bring up their five children. I knew I had to get away. So I made an excuse that I was feeling ill and grabbed my suitcase and left.

ෂ

A short while later, I stood watching the buses pull in and out of the bus station. They arrived and departed every minute or two, carrying people to destinations and places far better than where I stood now. It wouldn't be long before the Aberdeen bus was here. I couldn't wait to leave Dundee.

Dundee had been a disaster almost from the word go. There was nothing I would miss about the place. But my future still looked bleak and uncertain. I spent the last of my money on a ticket and now I was penniless and alone, without a friend or a job or a home. I couldn't sink much lower. I lifted up my eyes towards the sky where the sun was trying to break through dark clouds. What would tomorrow bring? There was no answer. I shuddered with the cold.

Epilogue

How the decades have flown by. The 16-year-old girl of long ago has all but vanished. Yet, I still see her occasionally, walking alone and homeless but with a spirit refusing to bow down or give up.

She was lucky to survive. God forbid, if she hadn't, then I wouldn't be here many years later, writing about the hard lonely road she walked down. The trials and tribulations, more than enough to fill another book, continued long after Dundee was just a distant memory.

Eight years, two marriages and five children later, she finally found the home she was looking for. She shares it with John, her partner for thirty years. And with the happy ending came greater understanding and the realisation she was never truly alone, even in the darkest of moments.

A power, a force, call it what you will, walked with her, unseen most of the time. Now and again it showed itself in the form of visions or help and guidance. Otherwise, would the taxi driver have been there to save her? I don't think so.

Writing about my experiences was probably one of the hardest things I've ever had to do in my life. I didn't want to remember them. They lay buried inside me for years. Yet, I knew one day I'd have to put pen to paper and share my experiences with others.

I'm glad I did. For if just one person going through a dark period in their life feels inspired to keep on going, then it's been well worth it. The bad times really do come to an end, sooner or later. I am living proof of that.

I've neglected everyone and everything writing this book and I'm really sorry. But it couldn't be helped. Once started, I had to finish it. I don't think I had a choice in the matter. The young girl of long ago cried out once more to be heard and I couldn't turn my back and just ignore her and walk away, like so many did in the past.

The road is still there, full of ups and downs. But she no longer walks down it alone for which I am truly thankful.